Eliza Julia Flower

Eliza Julia Flower, 1855, by D. Roster, courtesy of the Chicago Historical Society

George Flower, 1855, by D. Roster, courtesy of the Chicago Historical
Society

Eliza Julia Flower

Letters of an English Gentlewoman:
Life on the Illinois-Indiana Frontier

1817–1861

Janet R. Walker

and

Richard W. Burkhardt

BALL   STATE   UNIVERSITY

Muncie, Indiana

Library of Congress Card Catalog Number: 91-76613

ISBN 0-937994-20-0

90397 up

Table of Contents

Illustrations viii

Acknowledgments ix

Introduction 1

Chapter 1   *Thus ends the black chapter of our history* 27

Chapter 2   *This is the Country for a poor labouring Man*
  with a large Family 41

Chapter 3   *[The Ohio River is] the grand thoroughfare*
  to all the Western States 59

Chapter 4   *I have educated them as far as I am capable* 73

Chapter 5   *American females have a sleight of hand*
  in getting through house-work of all
  kinds without apparent labour 87

Chapter 6   *The business of the merchants is very*
  extensive 105

Chapter 7   *[George Flower had] the unwaning love*
  of a high-minded warm hearted,
  spirited woman 125

Epilogue 147

Appendix A: Descendants of Richard Flower 154

Appendix B: Descendants of Mordecai Andrews 155

Appendix C: Town of Albion Articles of Agreement 156

Notes 160

Selected Bibliography 178

Illustrations

Eliza Julia Flower . . . . frontispiece

George Flower . . . . frontispiece

Map of Illinois 1824 6

The English Prairie 7

Map of the Environs of Albion. 9

Morris Birkbeck at his desk 12

Title page of the Swedish Edition of Birkbeck's *Notes
on a Journey* 13

Title page of Birkbeck's *Extracts from a Supplementary
Letter from the Illinois—and a Reply to
William Cobbett, Esq.* 14

Cauliflower Lodge 18

Party on horseback leaving Park House for
a ride on the Prairie 39

George Flower 52

Title page of *The Navigator*. 62

Map from *The Navigator* 63

Park House . . . . opposite page 88

Park House . . . . opposite page 89

A stone house in Albion 99

Letter and signature of Eliza Julia 121

Rappite Dormitory #2. 128

Eliza Julia Flower 134

Medallion holding a picture of Eliza Julia and
a lock of her hair 139

Tombstones of George and Eliza Julia Flower 145

Monument at the site of Park House 148

Acknowledgments

FIRST AMONG THE MANY to whom we wish to express our indebtedness is Dorothy Durland (Mrs. Edson) Robinson of Watertown, New York, who is John Rutt Andrews's great-great-granddaughter and in whose family Eliza Julia's letters have been carefully preserved and passed from generation to generation. Without Mrs. Robinson's generosity in sharing these letters with us we would not have been able to write this book. We are also grateful to Mrs. Patricia Flower Martin, from whom we received permission to publish letters from Eliza Julia to her son Camillus and letters between the brothers and sisters who were Eliza Julia's children.

We are especially grateful to Dr. David Rice, president of the University of Southern Indiana, without whom we would never have met and discovered the interest in Eliza Julia that we share. His continued interest in our work has encouraged us. Foremost among those who assisted us are Aline Cook and Rosemary Alsop, librarians, Workingmen's Institute, New Harmony, Indiana, and Josephine M. Elliott, former librarian, University of Southern Indiana. Carol Shaw, Albion Public Library; Laurel G. Bowen, former curator, and Cheryl Scherring, current curator of the Manuscript Division of the Illinois State Historical Library; Ralph Pugh, assistant curator of the Manuscript Division of the Chicago Historical Society; John Hoffman of the Illinois Historical Survey, Urbana; and Jeff Douglass and Carley R. Robison, Knox College Library, were gracious and always accommodating.

Our thanks, too, to members of the Department of History, Ball State University: Sharon Seager, Bruce Geelhoed, Dwight Hoover, Anthony Edmonds, and Ray White, who gave their time to read and to criticize the manuscript. Thanks also to Dr. Kay Wagoner, professor of business education and office administration, and Dr. Casey Tucker, assistant director of the university computing services, for guidance in the operation of the word processor, and to the Ball State Office of Publication Services for producing the book.

Without the support and cooperation of Eliza Julia Flower's descendants, Janet Flower of Los Angeles, William Fordham Flower of Larchmont, New York, and William Flower of Sunnyside, Washington, and their family stories, we would not have captured half so well the personality and distinguishing qualities of Eliza Julia.

We are grateful to the Ball State University Faculty Publications and Intellectual Properties Committee for recommending the publication of this book and to Provost C. Warren Vander Hill for acting on the recommendation.

We are also grateful for the courtesy of the following:

The Chicago Historical Society for permission to publish portraits of Eliza Julia Flower and George Flower and quotations from letters in the Flower Family Papers.

The Harvard University Library for permission to publish quotations from the *Bulletin* "The Nashoba Plan for removing the Evil of Slavery: Letters of Frances and Camilla Wright 1820–1829," Cecelia Helena Payne-Gaposchkin.

The Illinois State Historical Society for permission to publish quotations from Flower family letters, *Journal* articles, and the picture on page 99.

The Indiana Historical Society for permission to publish quotations from a letter of Robert Dale Owen in the New Harmony Collection.

Knox College Archives for permission to publish an 1824 map and five photographs.

Muséum d'Histoire Naturelle du Havre for permission to publish sketches by Chalres Alexandre Lesueur.

Mrs. Dennis Flower, C. B. E. Warwickshire, England, for permission to quote from *Great Aunt Sarah's Diary.*

Special thanks to Dorothy Burkhardt and B. P. Walker for their several contributions, as well as unflagging encouragement and patience.

Introduction

LIFE ON THE ILLINOIS FRONTIER in the early nineteenth century was exciting to a degree that is scarcely imaginable to persons living in the late twentieth century. The excitement stemmed from the hopes and promises of a new and better life, not only for the Americans who pushed westward from the eastern shores, but also perhaps even more for the immigrants from England and Europe. The policies of the United States government that made land relatively available encouraged the dream and the promise of a better life in a new land, with the result that immigration, land sales, and land speculation flourished.

The immigrants paid a dear price for this new life. Before they reached Illinois, they had already endured a six- to eight-week passage across the Atlantic Ocean in a sailing vessel and another eight- to ten-week journey by horse, wagon, and riverboat. Their travels might well be classified as ordeals. When those who survived the journey arrived in Indiana and Illinois in 1817, they found that as recently as 1814 Indians had sacked and burned frontier settlements. Although the Indian conflicts were over, settlers believed their isolation on the prairies to be precarious, if not actually dangerous. While following the will-o'-the-wisp of the promises of a new and better life, the frontiersman often stumbled over the daily drudgery of carving a farm out of the woods in the wilderness or breaking and draining the prairie sod. The pioneers, men and women, awoke each morning to some new surprise, some new problem to solve. The major avenues of making a living were restricted to hunting and farming until there were enough people living near each other to require the specialized services of a blacksmith, doctor, tanner, or tavern keeper. Malaria and fevers routinely interrupted, and sometimes ended, the lives of the people. Of the numerous children who were born, many did not survive to adulthood. Some who tried life on the frontier succeeded in finding their dreams, but many left to return to more settled centers. The gravestones testify to the numbers who died along the way or during the early years of the settlement.

One of the important stories of hope, excitement, despair, and disappointment is that of the English Settlement in Edwards County, Illinois. Two Englishmen, Morris Birkbeck and George Flower, inspired by the promise and hope of a better life in America, came with their families to Illinois, where they founded the towns of Wanborough and Albion on land that came to be called the English Prairie. The contributions of the two men to Illinois and to the Midwest were significant, indeed in some ways pivotal in the history of Illinois.

Englishmen like Birkbeck and Flower were willing to leave their homes and face the rigors of the frontier because of the difficulties of life in England and Europe at the beginning of the nineteenth century. Social and economic unrest that followed the nearly thirty years between the French Revolution and the Napoleonic Wars were strong forces pushing people to emigrate. To make matters worse, the dislocations brought about by the Industrial Revolution, a series of crop failures, and an absence of leadership from the British government in domestic affairs all combined to make life in England intolerable for many. George Flower, mildest of commentators, wrote, "this state of affairs produced great uneasiness."[1]

These forces pushing people away from England were enhanced by the pull of the hope of a better life in the new United States of America. By 1817–18 the desire to leave England affected hundreds of Englishmen. Societies were formed to encourage emigration to all parts of the British empire. Australia, Canada, and the Cape of Good Hope all had their Emigrant Aid Societies and a regular line between England and each colony. As early as 1816, editorials in English newspapers deplored the "ruinous drain of the most useful part of the kingdom, as tillers of the soil, artisans and even some wealthy people left England."[2]

The United States of America was the most attractive destination for dissatisfied Englishmen because the great majority of Americans shared the same English language and traditions with them. The history of the settlement of America and the recently won freedom from the oppressive British rule made the United States a more favored choice for English emigrants than any other English-speaking area of the world. In the United States land could be purchased at reasonable prices in the East, and in the West it was almost free. Because skilled labor was in great demand, the opportunities for farmers and artisans were myriad.

Richard Flower, father of George, was a prosperous brewer and landowner from Hertfordshire whose estate, Marden Hill, was near Hertford. In the early nineteenth century, Marden had been a favorite gathering place for the liberals and reformers of the day. Richard's elder brother, Benjamin Flower, a radical newspaper editor, and William Cobbett, author of *Rural Rides* and perhaps the best known of the pamphleteers, were typical visitors at Marden. The collapse of the agricultural economy after the Napoleonic Wars, the imposition by the government of the malt tax on the liquor trade, the poor laws, and particularly the restrictions placed on religious dissenters were irksome to the Flower family. These government policies and the tithes imposed by the established church were topics of endless debate by the politicians, landowners, writers, friends, and acquaintances of the Flowers who often sat at Marden over a glass of madeira or a cup of tea discussing the hopelessness of the future in old England.

Seeking an alternative to the troubled life in England, George, eldest son of Richard, with Morris Birkbeck, a well-to-do farmer and family friend, journeyed into France in 1815 to examine agricultural practices and the conditions of farming life there. They were assisted in their investigations by General LaFayette, who demonstrated a real interest in their venture. After careful study they concluded that France was not the place to which they would wish to emigrate because they disliked what they thought were the repressive roles of the church and the military in French society.

In 1816 George set out for America, hoping to find a place for a future home. His mission was to examine a variety of places in America so that he could advise his father about the desirability of leaving England for the new world. He traveled to New York and Philadelphia and through Pennsylvania, Ohio, and Virginia. He met people like Thomas Jefferson, to whom he had a letter of introduction from General LaFayette. Mr. Jefferson, in turn, introduced him to other Virginia planters and farmers from whom he gleaned much information about affairs in America and American farming. By coincidence, while George was visiting the family of Colonel John Coles in Albermarle, Virginia, Coles's son Edward was in England extolling the western prairies to Morris Birkbeck. During this time George wrote regularly to both his father Richard and to their friend Birkbeck. George liked what he found and encouraged his father to join him in a new life in America. Richard ultimately accepted that advice.

How much was planned and how much happened by chance remains uncertain, but at the time George was preparing to return home to report to his father on his explorations, he learned that Birkbeck and his family had landed in Norfolk. George hastened to meet them, and after the reunion of the two friends, they decided to proceed together at once to the western country.

On the journey to Illinois, Birkbeck had quite a large party with him: four of his children, Charles, Bradford, Eliza, and Prudence; George Flower's cousin, Elias Pym Fordham, an engineer; an orphan girl named Elizabeth Garton; a servant boy, Gillard; and a beautiful young lady, a good friend of the Birkbeck family, Eliza Julia Andrews, aged twenty-five, daughter of the Reverend Mordecai Andrews of Eigeshall, Essex.

The route that George and the Birkbeck party, except for Fordham, traveled took them from Petersburg, where they cleared customs, by steamer to Richmond, Virginia, and on to Washington by coach. From Washington they made their way by stagecoach to Fredericksburg, Maryland, and to McConnelsburg, Pennsylvania, on the Pennsylvania State Road. Here traveling became more difficult. Because there were no stages to be had, they walked the Pennsylvania Pike from McConnelsburg to Pittsburgh. This story is confirmed by a letter written on June 3, 1817, from George Flower to Judge Peters of Belmont, Pennsylvania: "The first day was hot—we walked 10 miles, the second 17, the third 20: we arrived at Pittsburgh on Sunday last after a walk of 120 miles."[3]

In his book *Notes on a Journey in America*, Morris Birkbeck described the western tide of emigration of which their group was a small part:

We have now fairly turned our backs on the old world, and find ourselves in the very stream of emigration. Old America seems to be breaking up and moving westward. We are seldom out of sight, as we travel on this grand track towards the Ohio, of family groups behind and before us,—The New Englanders, they say, may be known by the cheerful air of their women advancing in front of the vehicle; the Jersey people by their being fixed steadily within it; whilst the Pennsylvanians creep lingering behind, as though regretting the homes they have left. —Often the back of the poor pilgrim bears all his effects, and his wife follows barefooted, bending under the hopes of the family.[4]

Elias Pym Fordham assumed the responsibility for the baggage, which he took up Chesapeake Bay on a hired schooner and across the Allegheny Mountains on three sturdy wagons. The way west beyond Pittsburgh could be taken by water, which was the route followed by Fordham. He loaded the baggage on flatboats or arks and floated them down the Ohio River. At Pittsburgh, Birkbeck and Flower chose an alternate route: they decided that it would be better to make the trip overland on horseback in order to see more of the country than to take the more common route down the Ohio River by flatboat. For the cross-country ride, each member of the group was equipped with a "sturdy horse, a large blanket on the seat of the saddle for the rider, a pair of well-filled saddle bags, all secured by a surcingle, a greatcoat or cloak, with umbrella strapped behind."[5] In this manner the party traveled through Ohio to Cincinnati. Here they met Mr. Sloo, the register of the new land office at Shawneetown, Illinois, who agreed to guide them through Indiana, a much less settled country. The party, being young, with the exception of Morris Birkbeck, and all well mannered, well educated, and congenial, seemed to enjoy the trip despite the

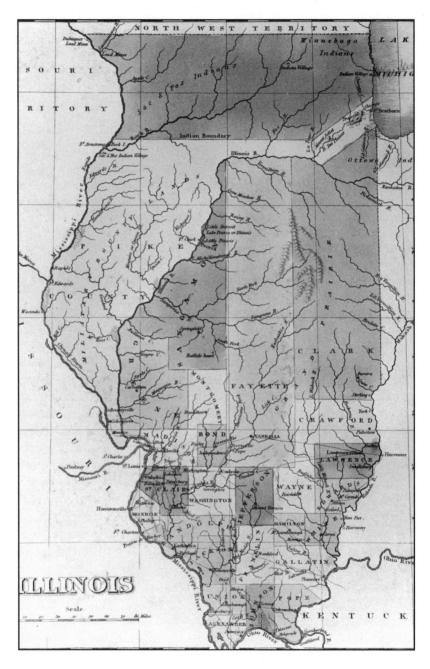

Map of Illinois, 1824, by Finley, courtesy of Knox College Library

Sketch of the English Prairie, by Charles Alexandre LeSueur, courtesy of Muséum d'Histoire Naturelle du Havre

physical difficulties, the violent storms, the black mud, the unbroken gloomy forests, and the filthy cabins that served as taverns.

Having established a temporary home at Princeton, Indiana, Flower and Birkbeck inquired about the prairies in Illinois and were surprised to find that on the east bank of the Wabash River, where travelers were arriving daily, little seemed to be known of the lands across the Wabash on the west bank. George Flower and Morris and Bradford Birkbeck set off to explore the Illinois country. They had been advised earlier by Mr. Sloo to inquire for the Boltenhouse Prairie. After a grueling seven hours on horseback they found it. George wrote,

A few steps more and a beautiful prairie suddenly opened to our view. At first we only received the impressions of its general beauty. With longer gaze, all its distinctive features were revealed, lying in profound repose under the warm light of an afternoon's summer sun. Its indented and irregular outline of wood, its varied surface interspersed with clumps of oaks of centuries' growth, its tall grass, with seed stalks from six to ten feet high, like tall and slender reeds waving in a gentle breeze, the whole presenting a magnificence of park scenery, complete from the hand of Nature, and unrivaled by the same sort of scenery by European art. For once the reality came up to the picture of the imagination. Our station was in the wood, on a rising ground; from it, a descent of about a hundred yards to the valley of the prairie, about a quarter of a mile wide, extending to the base of a majestic slope, rising upward for a full half mile, crowned by groves of noble oaks. A little to the left, the eye wandered up a long stretch of prairie for three miles, into which projected hills and slopes, covered with rich grass and decorated with compact clumps of full grown trees, from four to eight in each clump. From beneath the broken shade of the wood, with our arms raised above our brows, we gazed long and steadily, drinking in the beauties of the scene which had been so long the object of our search.[6]

The broad and fertile grasslands that gave to Illinois the name "The Prairie State" stretched from Edwards County, where Birkbeck and Flower settled, north beyond the Illinois border into Wisconsin as well as into the states farther west.

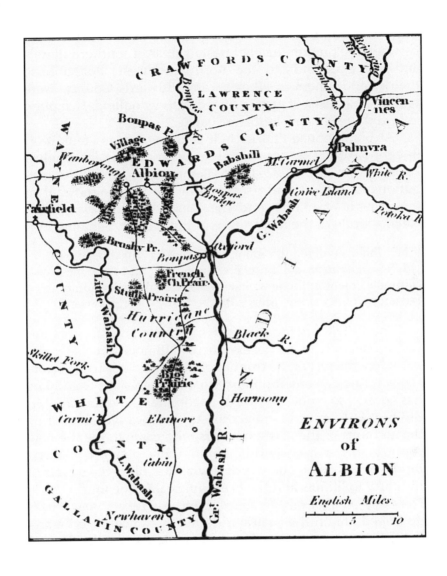

Map of the Environs of Albion, 1822, by Hall, courtesy of the Newberry Library, Chicago

Edwards County lay in what geographers call a transition line between the predominately forested areas of southern Illinois and the grasslands to the north and west. Boltenhouse Prairie, and others in what became Edwards County, were parklike expanses of grass, fringed with woodland, that often followed the streams and river banks.[7]

At Boltenhouse Prairie their settlement plans took root; Boltenhouse Prairie soon came to be known as the English Prairie. From 1817 to 1825 the settlement grew, and the contributions its leaders and its people made were significant in the growth of Illinois and the West. The historian Allen Nevins wrote of the importance of the English Settlement,

When Illinois entered the union in 1818, of its 35,000 people the old French *habitants* still numbered one tenth; and the richest cultural element in the new State was the British community in Edwards County under Morris Birkbeck and George Flower.[8]

The British community of which Nevins wrote was important not only to the development of Illinois, but also to the growth of the rest of the frontier of the time. "It is true," wrote William Faux, a contemporary, "that no man since Columbus has done so much towards peopling America as Mr. Birkbeck."[9] Interest in emigration to America was fanned by the accounts of the many travelers who came to see the new country and who went home to write about it. Morris Birkbeck was an eloquent writer who described the travels of his party to Illinois and the beautiful prairies he found there. His *Notes on a Journey in America* and his *Letters from Illinois* described life on the prairie in terms that encouraged many English and some Europeans to emigrate to the United States.[10] Both books were read avidly in England and in Europe. Thirty different editions of his *Notes* and *Letters* appeared, including several translations into languages other than English. From 1817 until after 1830 the English Settlement in Edwards County, Illinois, was internationally known and discussed. A receptive audience for *Notes* had been created by the social and economic hardships of life in England and Europe already described.

A great literary struggle ensued between those who objected to Birkbeck's writings and those who were favorable to his accounts. Not all travelers praised what they found when they arrived in America. Some complained that they had been misled by glowing reports of the new world. Writers like William Cobbett and others filled journals such as *The Quarterly Review* with complaints about Birkbeck's description of life in America. Fearing punishment for his bitter attacks on the English government, Cobbett had fled from England to settle on the East Coast of the United States. He thought that it was unnecessary for Englishmen to go farther west than where he was, and he attacked his former friends, Birkbeck and the Flowers, with his sharp pen as vigorously as he had attacked the government of England. In reply, others wrote articles, particularly in *North American Review,* favoring Birkbeck. The debate between Birkbeck's critics and his supporters only increased the interest of potential emigrants in America. An extensive body of travel descriptions became the major focus of public interest in the United States and in England. As the fame of the English Prairie spread, interest in moving to the Middle West increased; the English Settlement was the magnet that drew many travelers of the time to see what the West was really like.[11] In his compendium of accounts of travel in America, Solon J. Buck writes,

One of the most interesting movements in American colonization is the English Settlement established by Morris Birkbeck and George Flower in Edwards County. The books written by the founders and other members of the Settlement are numerous and frequently ran through many editions; while nearly every traveler who visited Illinois from 1818 to 1825 made it a point to see the English Settlement and give his opinions of it in his book.[12]

There was a legitimate basis for misunderstanding what life on the frontier in America was really like. George Flower, addressing the fact that many immigrants were discouraged by the realities of the life they found, explained,

I found some difficulty in giving a truthful picture to the Englishman who had never been out of England—You tell of a log house. The only houses he has seen are buildings with plastered or papered walls, with ceiling and floors, with halls, passages, cellars, and attics, and each room is furnished with a good chimney and hearth. The simple log house he can scarcely realize.[13]

Wanborough
Illinois

M. Birkbeck

London. Pub.d by T. & W. Boone 480. Strand. 1825.

Printed by C. Hullmandel.

Sketch of Morris Birkbeck at his desk, courtesy of Knox College Library

NYBYGGARNE

i

NORDAMERIKA,

Deras Öden och Utsigter.

En teckning efter Naturen;
af en Engelsman,
jemte Engelska omdömen och betraktel-
ser, föranledda deraf.

STOCKHOLM, 1818.
Tryckt i CEDERBORGSKA Boktryckeriet.

Title page of Birkbeck's *Notes on a Journey*, in Swedish, 1818, courtesy of Knox College Library

EXTRACTS

FROM A

SUPPLEMENTARY LETTER

FROM THE ILLINOIS,

DATED JANUARY 31st, 1819.

—

ADDRESS

TO

British Emigrants

ARRIVING IN THE EASTERN PORTS.

JULY 13th, 1819.

—

REPLY

TO

WILLIAM COBBETT, ESQ.

JULY 31st, 1819.

—

BY MORRIS BIRKBECK.

—

NEW-YORK:

PUBLISHED BY C. WILEY AND CO. 3 WALL-STREET.

J. Seymour, printer.

1819.

Title page of Birkbeck's *Extracts from a Supplementary Letter From the Illinois—and a Reply to William Cobbett, Esq., 1819,* courtesy of Knox College Library

The critical contribution to the development of Illinois by the work of Flower and especially that of Birkbeck in preventing Illinois from becoming a slave state is generally recognized.[14] Until 1825 most of the settlers in Illinois were from southern states and brought with them the custom of slavery or, if they had no slaves themselves, a general sympathy for it. The English, on the other hand, like Birkbeck, who was of Quaker origin, and Flower, a Unitarian, were actively opposed to slavery. In the political test of 1824 the English successfully persuaded enough American settlers to keep Illinois a free state. Birkbeck was a gifted writer who, through his pamphlets and letters to newspapers under the pen names of "Jonathan Freeman" and "O," was a very effective advocate. George Flower made innumerable trips on horseback around the settled parts of the state persuasively campaigning for the anti-slavery vote.

Birkbeck and Flower greatly influenced farming practices on the Illinois prairie. Early American settlers had shunned the prairies because they thought that the best land was where the trees grew, and since timber was needed for building, most early settlers chose to live in the forested areas. Those who attempted to farm the prairies found that prairie sod was so thick that it was difficult to till and that drainage was a continuing problem. Serious agriculturists, Birkbeck and Flower showed others how to farm the Illinois prairie by introducing advanced concepts of animal husbandry and techniques for draining wetlands.

Still another of their contributions was the introduction of a more cultured manner of living. Life on the frontier was generally primitive. The English brought with them glass for their windows, pianos, books, and other hallmarks of a more civilized life that they had left behind. Their life-styles helped to change the way other people lived.

Despite all this, the English Settlement did not ultimately meet the aspirations of its founders. Birkbeck and Flower hoped to attract other persons like themselves, successful farmers in England who, hobbled by social and economic restrictions, would come to America with the resources to buy land from them. They also hoped to attract working men and women whose artisan skills would help them get started until subsequently they too would become landowners. More of the latter than the former came to Illinois, and the numbers failed to increase as rapidly as Birkbeck and Flower had hoped.

The economic conditions of the time worked against the rapid growth of the English Settlement. In its early years Illinois grew rapidly, but not at the right times and places for the two Englishmen. In 1800 it was a part of the Indiana Territory. In 1809 it became the Illinois Territory, and in 1818 it achieved statehood. When the threat of Indian attacks related to the War of 1812 was removed, the population grew rapidly. By 1814 there was an economic boom underway caused by the crop failures in Europe, which increased the demand for American agricultural products. Liberal credit arrangements for the purchase of land also contributed to the boom. In 1800 the minimum purchase of land was 320 acres; this amount was reduced to 160 acres in 1804, and by 1817 a limited number of 80-acre tracts were available.

Unfortunately for Birkbeck and Flower the conditions that had promoted growth changed sharply by 1818. The economic boom crested in 1816–17. Better harvests in Europe decreased the markets for American farmers, and the interest in purchasing land declined even though the purchase price of $2 an acre was reduced to $1.25. Illinois historian Pease noted, "Very little land was bought in Illinois for ten years thereafter."[15] Those ten years, 1818–25, were critical years for the success of the new settlement.

Adverse economic conditions were not the only hindrance to the growth of the community on the English Prairie that made it less than the dreams of the two leaders. Lack of fruition was due in part to a falling-out between them. The differences between them led Birkbeck to build a little village of his own, which he named Wanborough, less than two miles away from Flower's village, which was called Albion. The story of the split between the two was embroidered by some of the critics of the English Settlement, which contributed further to the detriment of both villages.

The exact reason for the division between Birkbeck and Flower is impossible to establish, for neither of them ever wrote about it. Many people believe that Eliza Julia Andrews was the cause. What is verifiable is that while traveling from the East Coast to Illinois, Birkbeck, then fifty-three years old and a widower, had made a proposal of marriage to Miss Andrews, twenty-eight years his junior. She refused his proposal, but not long after that she did accept a proposal of marriage from the twenty-nine-year-old George Flower. George and Eliza Julia were married in Vincennes on July 15, 1817, by Elihu Stout, J.P., and since it was Morris Birkbeck who gave the bride away, there appeared to be no major rift between Birkbeck and Flower at that time. After the ceremony they traveled on to Princeton together. After George and Eliza Julia returned from a brief wedding trip to the nearby Shaker community of Busro, the whole party stayed briefly at the tavern of Basil Brown and then took a house in Princeton as a group with Eliza Julia Flower, the senior woman, in charge as housekeeper. It was from this base that George Flower and Morris and Bradford Birkbeck crossed the Wabash River to explore the Illinois country.

When they had found their prairie, Morris Birkbeck and George Flower agreed that the former would go to Shawneetown to enter their land claims, and Flower would return to England to recruit settlers and obtain money for their project. The newlyweds, unwilling to be parted any sooner than absolutely necessary, decided that Eliza Julia would travel with George to the eastern side of the Alleghenies, where she would await his return in the spring. In late September, after being in the western country slightly more than two months, they set out for Chambersburg, Pennsylvania. They traveled hard, nearly forty miles a day despite oppressive September heat and perilous flooding in Ohio of entire valleys, which made it impossible to distinguish rivers or deep lakes from backwater. It was a rugged trip for a woman in the early stages of pregnancy, even an excellent horsewoman with remarkable stamina. When they reached Chambersburg, George left Eliza Julia in the care of a Mrs. Hettick, tavernkeeper, whom they had met on their original

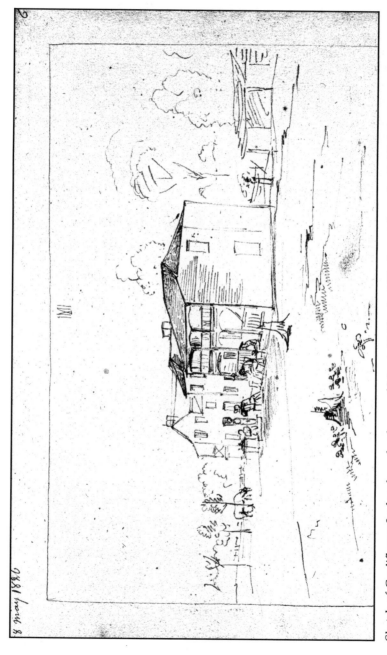

Sketch of Cauliflower Lodge, large log home of Morris Birkbeck at Wanborough on the English Prairie, May 1826, by Charles Alexandre LeSueur, courtesy of Muséum d'Histoire Naturelle du Havre

trip west. There she spent the winter and gave birth to their first child.

When Flower, with his wife and child, returned to the English Settlement in the spring of 1818, he had accomplished all he had set out to do; he had arranged for the publication of Morris Birkbeck's book, *Notes on a Journey in America*, in both Philadelphia and England; he had raised the necessary funds for Birkbeck to buy more land; he had recruited two parties of immigrants, totalling more than eighty persons, for the prairie, and he had assisted his father, Richard Flower, and his family to move to America. Upon his return, when George went to report the results of his trip to Birkbeck, his former friend announced that he would never speak to him again. No reason was given for this action. Whatever the cause, and there were surmises of causes other than that of George's marriage to Eliza Julia, the difference between the two founders unquestionably handicapped the growth of the settlement.

In Albion, as in some other frontier communities, there was friction among the first settlers. The original proprietors, who had laid out the town and invested in its development, disagreed about the details of its growth to the point of taking legal action against each other, so that during what should have been the formative years of the settlement some potential settlers chose to find homes elsewhere to escape involvement in the disputes. Many of them were deflected to other settlements along the Ohio River, and some of them moved to the Utopian community of New Harmony in Indiana.[16] Dr. Charles Pugsley, one of the original settlers, was recognized as an able physician, but he proved to be a contentious member of the community and was especially antagonistic toward Richard Flower. He brought many suits against the Flowers before the proprietors, of which he was one, broke up. William Owen, one of Robert Owen's sons, writing of a meeting with Pugsley, said,

Dr. Pugley [sic]— He said he was very sorry for the differences existing at Albion and he wished he had yielded to Mr. Flower; but he opposed him because he (Richard Flower) wished to be the great man and he (Pugsley) could not brook that.[17]

When Dr. Pugsley moved away a major source of friction within the community was gone. The years after 1825 were peaceful owing largely to the influence of Walter Mayo. Mayo had come to Albion in 1818 as a schoolteacher and soon became county clerk, judge, and treasurer. During his thirty-nine years of public service he gained universal respect for his ability to resolve conflicts even before they came to his court. It was said that "no lawyer could earn a living in Edwards County during Mayo's time."[18]

More important in limiting the growth of the English Settlement than anything mentioned thus far was the rise of New Harmony. The English settlers at Wanborough and Albion were greatly assisted in their formative years by the existence of the Rappite colony at Harmonie, less than twenty miles away on the Indiana side of the Wabash River. Because of the industry and abilities of George Rapp and his disciples, Harmonie was an established community from which the English purchased supplies and equipment. After some ten years in Indiana at Harmonie, George Rapp decided to take his people back to Pennsylvania and build another new community. George Flower's father, Richard, was commissioned by Rapp to offer the entire Harmonie property for sale to Robert Owen, a Scottish textile manufacturer and reformer. Donald MacDonald recorded in his diary that Rapp and Owen arrived at agreements about the sale and purchase of Harmonie at Richard Flower's home, Park House, on 28 December 1814, and William Owen wrote that the final papers were signed there on 3 January 1815.[19]

At New Lanark, Scotland, Owen had developed the concepts that if his employees were well paid and had decent housing and proper education for their children they would be both happier and more productive workers. The implementation of these ideas, unusual for their time, brought Owen great wealth and notoriety in Scotland and England. Encouraged by his successes with social reform, he was eager to try them out on a larger scale involving an entire community. Harmonie was made to order as the place to launch New Harmony. To attract settlers, Owen offered newcomers an equal share in the new community and the promise of a new social order. Some of the English at Albion and thirteen families from Wanborough left the English Settlement to join Owen's experiment. Not only did the settlement lose population; it also lost the world's attention as New Harmony gained notoriety. As the social experiment at Owen's New Harmony quickly unfolded, the world's attention was drawn from the English Settlement, which was less frequently mentioned and visited less after 1825 than it had been earlier.

John A. Jakle, historian-geographer, examined 387 travel books written between 1740 and 1860, identified the travelers' routes and destinations, and grouped the data by decades; he found that during the first years of the nineteenth century many visitors came to Albion, but in the period 1830–40 there were none.[20] New Harmony had eclipsed the English Settlement.

The final curtailment of the hopes for the growth of Albion came with the founding of Chicago and other northern Illinois cities; these developments overshadowed events on the English Prairie after 1825. After the opening of the Erie Canal in 1825 a flood of immigration came to the northern and western lands of Illinois. Forty-thousand settlers went west on the Erie Canal the first year that it was in operation. Historian Roy Billington wrote, "Now the Great Lakes, not the Ohio River, formed the pathway toward the setting sun."[21] The population of the state, which was 150,000 in 1830, increased threefold to 475,000 by 1840,[22] but the increase was not in Edwards County. The great majority of these people now lived in the northern part of the state, and in response to this shift in population the capital was moved north from Vandalia to Springfield. As a result, southeastern Illinois and the English Prairie disappeared from the public eye.

Morris Birkbeck drowned in 1825 while crossing the Fox River after a visit with Robert Owen. Most persons writing about the English Settlement conclude their stories with Birkbeck's death. Birkbeck's village of Wanborough disappeared, and all the Birkbeck children moved away. The Flower family remained in Albion, the town George and his father had built, and their children lived in the area throughout the century. Albion became the county seat of Edwards County in 1821, and as English settlers continued to come to Illinois it was known as Little Britain. George and Eliza Julia

Flower lived on the outskirts of Albion until 1849, when they moved to New Harmony.

The first years of the English Settlement, 1817–25, are well documented, but the next quarter-century, in which the Flowers continued to be active, is not. From Eliza Julia's letters one can begin to learn something of life in southeastern Illinois after the excitement of the opening of the frontier had passed and when Albion was no longer center stage. The first twelve letters included in this collection were written to her nephew, John Rutt Andrews, between 13 January 1833 and 2 February 1837. Andrews had emigrated from England, where he had been apprenticed to a needlemaker, to New York City, where he worked as a jeweler. He married an American woman and subsequently brought two of his brothers, Charles and George, to America. It was for the advancement of these brothers that he sought out his aunt in Illinois. The letters written to her children after 1837 fill a gap in the information about the region. Eliza Julia reveals through them the kind of life she led as an English gentlewoman who became an American in the backwoods of Illinois and Indiana in the early 1800s. The author of these letters was an unusual person; to see southeastern Illinois through her eyes one must learn something about her.

Eliza Julia's life in Illinois did not have an auspicious beginning. When she and George and their new baby came to Illinois from Chambersburg, Pennsylvania, they not only found their former friend Birkbeck estranged, but also learned that he had failed to provide any kind of accommodation for them as he had promised, nor had he purchased for them additional acreage, as he had also promised and for which they had sent him money. They came back to the prairie to find they had only a primitive log cabin that cousin Elias Pym Fordham had built for them on their land. This first home was a cabin with a clapboard roof, log walls, and a puncheon floor with a hole where the hearth was to be. The nearest water was one-half mile away. The extreme difficulties of this rugged beginning, coupled with the change in climate, resulted in severe illness—the common ailment of all newcomers, the ague. The whole family became ill and were nursed by Eliza Julia.

George Flower recorded her unflagging devotion to her family:

We were carried through this period of trial by the unremitting labor and self-sacrifice of my wife.—Sustained in her unremitting labors by unbounded devotion to her family and a high sense of duty to all within her reach, her spirit and her power seemed to rise above the manifold trials by which she was surrounded. And thus we were saved from probable death or certain dispersion. The incessant labor of the mother told on the infant at the breast. It sickened and died.[23]

This instance of caring and devotion in spite of the death of her first child, Emma, was but one of the many instances of Eliza Julia's remarkable courage and stamina. She bore another little Emma in 1819, and over the subsequent years a dozen more children, including twins in 1829 and in 1832. The births of her last two children, Richard, 1834, and Benjamin, 1835, occurred during the time of her correspondence with her nephew, John. Eight of her fourteen children lived to adulthood.

The original cabin in which George and Eliza Julia lived eventually became a most interesting series of seven log cabins combined into one attractive large house, extremely comfortable, graciously accoutered, and lavishly furnished. It was appropriately called "Prairie House." It also had a one-hundred-foot-square stable yard completely enclosed by two-story log buildings.

While George and Richard, his father, gave their time, energies, and money to the town of Albion, Eliza Julia devoted herself to caring for her husband and their children. George spent much time away from home on town business and his own or his father's animal husbandry and agricultural pursuits. On rare occasions Eliza Julia traveled with him, but the responsibilities of her household and her frequent pregnancies kept her for the most part at home on the English Prairie. From her letters it is clear that she loved her family and her prairie; if she ever longed to return to England, as did many of her compatriots, she never let it be known.

Seeking a clearer picture of Eliza Julia, one finds a self-description in her letter to John Andrews dated 1 September 1833:

When I left England I was a blooming girl, now I am an old woman, the mother of 12 children, grey headed and almost toothless. I am of a happy temperment and always have been and am now very healthy—my delight is in my home. I believe my husband doats on me, and if he doesn't I doat upon him—My dress is always black with a white turban! Now don't you thank me for this fine description of myself? I forgot to tell you that my age is 42 or 43 and I desire after this minute description of myself that if you should meet me in the streets of New York, that you will immediately salute me without any further introduction.

Notable in this self-portrait is Eliza Julia's assertion of the love she and her husband have for one another, a theme that is reiterated in many of her letters. Her directness on this subject sets her apart from many other women of her time, who did not reveal their intimate feelings publicly to comparative strangers. Born in 1792, Eliza Julia was forty-one years old in 1833, and she was not coy about her age. It is difficult to determine the accuracy of the self-description, for there are only a few pictures extant, most taken in her later years and none particularly flattering. It is not difficult to establish how she was seen by others. She was repeatedly described as a great beauty having dark locks with an auburn glint and flashing brown eyes. In 1818, fifteen years before she described herself to John, an English traveler and author had written, "the gay, graceful, modest hearty, anticipating kindness of this lady, makes every guest feel himself at home and loth to depart."[24]

Robert Dale Owen, son of Robert Owen, writing from New Harmony in 1854, described his neighbor, Mrs. Flower, to a friend in Indianapolis, as

quite a character—a high minded, warm-hearted, spirited woman. Even now, at sixty or near it, the mother of six or seven children, all of adult age, after a life of continued labor and renewed disappointment, she retains the vivacity and almost the cheerfulness of early youth. To the remains of great beauty she still joins a raciness of wit.[25]

In 1882, historian E. B. Washburne, who edited George Flower's *History of the English Settlement,* remembered Eliza Julia as follows:

Mrs. Flower was a woman of rare intelligence and excellent education to which she united an energetic character and a courageous spirit. An affectionate wife, a devoted mother, a kind friend, and a good neighbor, she proved herself in all relations of life a true and noble woman.[26]

A well-deserved place in history has already been given to her husband, George Flower, but, as is true of so many pioneer women, Eliza Julia's contributions are not well enough known.

Chapter 1

"Thus ends the black chapter of our history."

George Flower

E LIZA JULIA'S FIRST LETTER is a cautious one revealing little about herself or her life in Illinois.*

Near Albion

January 13, 1833

My dear John,

I recieved your letter dated Dec. 15th New York last Sunday 6th January and I am sorry I couldn't answer it by return of Post. I now write however, to say that I was very glad to hear from you and should like much to know all about you and your Brother Charles—and indeed about all your brothers and sisters and your mother for whom I always had a great regard and your poor father—who was ever a kind brother to me—I can hardly imagine that you whom I left in England a little boy—should be grown up a young man—and I hope a *Good Man*—I am pleased to see that you write a neat letter and should be still more pleased to see you in Person but as I cannot do that at present I desire as soon as you recieve this—that you will sit down and write me a full and particular account of yourself and Charles—what your prospects are—your views and wishes—what your habits of Life are and have been—what brought you to America in short—write all you wish me to know—of yourself and family—your sister Jemima and where is she etc etc—anything you write will come safely to my

*The original spelling, grammar, and punctuation have been retained in all quoted materials.

27

hands—We live 1 ½ miles from Albion the Town wh Mr. Flower and his father and some other Gentelmen founded some years since—it is a small place but on a remarkably healthy spot—and the country round is both healthy and beautiful—I must hear from you again before I describe to you our Farm and our mode of life—and my Husband and my Children—but this much I will say that I have a very happy home and your Uncle is so kind that he would do anything I wished to assist you Boys—and therefore it is that I wish you to be very particular and faithful in your account of yourselves. It may be that a City Life may suit your Education and your inclination—or it may be that a Country life such as we live might make you the most happy—describe your person—tell how tall you are and what your general health is tell me all that you have done in the way of business and what mode of life you would prefer if you had your choice—tell me what situation you are in at present—and how you are circumstanced for money and Cloaths and friends and so forth—Let Charles write me a few lines in your next letter—I write now to both of you—is the Charles Wray you speak of one of my sister Harriet Wrays Children or is it the Brother of her Husband? This will appear a strange letter to you but you must remember that altho you are my Nephew—yet that we are strangers to each other—and altho I am quite inclined to act towards you as towards relations whom I love—yet I have nearer and dearer ties in my own home than I have in the whole world besides—and I am very cautious how I propose anything for your advancement until I hear more about you and feel assured it would be for our mutual comfort and benifit—my Husband sends his kind wishes and my Children desire their Love to you both—I shall rejoice to recieve your next Letter and am

Your affectionate Aunt

Eliza J. Flower

P. S. If you can lay your hands upon that newspaper in wh you read "Recollections of Illinois" send it to us—address me by Post—

Mrs. George Flower
near Albion
Edwards County
Illinois

Remember me kindly to C. Wray be he relation or be he my friend.

From the postscript of her letter, it would appear that John had found his aunt from a chance reading of one of the many articles written in eastern newspapers about the English Settlement, and it may be assumed that John's letter was a complete and pleasant surprise to his aunt. Eliza Julia had been in America for sixteen years when the letter arrived, and there is no evidence that she had heard from any of her family since marrying George Flower. She must have been hungry for news of them.

John had apparently inquired about the prospects of sending his brother to Albion. Eliza Julia did report that Albion was a remarkably healthy place, which was an important observation considering the illness often present on the frontier. She began to describe the relationship between her husband and herself when she wrote that her husband was very kind and would probably help Charles if she wished it. Her admission of caution reflects her primary concern that nothing might upset her family's well-being. Part of Eliza Julia's caution stemmed from the fact that she had not seen John since he was a child. Thus it is understandable that she attempted to elicit more information about him and his brother, Charles.

Eliza Julia might well have been cautious about inviting strangers into her household, although she often had a great number of guests. Travelers in America came to see the English Settlement and later New Harmony, only twenty miles away. Richard and George Flower were openhanded with their hospitality. Since there were few inns in the area, many of the travelers visited Prairie House or Park House, the elder Flowers' home, and some stayed for weeks. Descriptions of life on the frontier extoll the hospitality of its people. Typically, the frontier family was far from the next settlers and welcomed the chance to meet and talk with visitors. The Flowers and the frontiersmen shared the values of hospitality, but the Flowers' view of hospitality did not spring from loneliness or isolation. Their hospitality was different from that of the frontiersmen because of the differences in their social and economic status and because of the Flowers' proximity to Albion. Visitors stayed for varying and often unpredictable lengths of time.

Not all of the visits to the Flowers could have been pleasant for the family. One, that of Fanny Wright and her sister Camilla in 1825, nearly ruined Eliza Julia's life.

Frances (Fanny) Wright was born in Scotland in 1795. Her mother died when she was two and a half years old, and Fanny moved to London, where she was brought up by her grandfather. There she enjoyed an unusual education for a female and became an advocate of equality for women and a supporter of the abolition of slavery. She eventually assailed most of the conventions of her time, specifically the convention of marriage, which she believed limited the fulfillment of women as persons. Her long acquaintance with General LaFayette, who introduced her to significant people in Europe and in America, enhanced her opportunities. In 1824, Frances Wright made her second trip to America, at which time she visited Thomas Jefferson and became obsessed with the problem of slavery. On this journey, as on many others, she was accompanied by her sister Camilla.

In early 1825, she heard Robert Owen, the new owner of New Harmony, speak in Washington. Because Owen's unconventional ideas struck sympathetic chords in her thinking, she traveled to New Harmony later that spring in search of him. While in New Harmony and Albion, she learned of George Flower's interest in anti-slavery activity.

Flower, distressed by the treatment of blacks in Illinois, had arranged for a group of six black families under the leadership of a white man to go to Haiti by way of the Mississippi through New Orleans. He equipped them with provisions and agricultural tools for the trip to their new home. It was March 1823, and emotions about blacks ran high in the port city of New Orleans. The would-be emigrants were all thrown into jail until Flower sent $360 to have them released. Eventually the group completed their voyage to Haiti, where they were so well received that other blacks subsequently followed.

George and his father, Richard, became interested in another means of ameliorating the lives of blacks, an interest they shared with Fanny Wright. Together they planned and later established an experimental community called Nashoba, near Memphis, Tennessee, where slaves could be freed, educated, and trained in useful skills. Quick to take action when an idea possessed her, Fanny left New Harmony and Albion in the summer of 1825 for New York City to raise money for Nashoba. In mid-July she met George Flower and his father, and they traveled west to Albion together. It was in the fall that George and Fanny set off for Nashville to seek the advice of Andrew Jackson. After talking with him, they proceeded to Memphis, where they purchased the property that was to be Nashoba.

Nashoba was an ambitious undertaking; some, including George's father, thought it hopelessly idealistic. Although Richard Flower was interested in the Nashoba project, he thought they would have been wiser to buy an already established plantation rather than to start a community in a wilderness. Nevertheless, he did support the work. He wrote to his other son, Edward, in England:

Camilla Wright is yet with us. The first flatboat has just embarked laden with corn, flour, a yoke of oxen and wagon, 2 horses, sundry furniture and implements of husbandry. Willing to hazard all the advantages of a new settlement which if it succeeds will be of the utmost importance to the well being of the human race. Three days sail on a steamboat from Shawneetown will bring us there. I am very anxious on account of their health, so far south in a new settlement, and believe they might have purchased out some cotton planter at a much cheaper rate than they can raise a new settlement, but there is something so infatuating in new settlements perhaps it arises from vanity in everyone supposing he can do everything better than any who have gone before him.[1]

In his next letter, Richard wrote, "George has just returned from Nashoba to Albion to get more supplies for the new settlement. He made the trip of 370 miles on horseback in 11 days."[2] On his way back to Nashoba late in December, George became ill at Flim's Ferry about twenty miles down river from Shawneetown. Alone and without help, he surely would have died had not word of his sickness reached Eliza Julia, who left her children and household responsibilities to rush to his side to nurse him back to health. The best account of this desperate situation occurs in a letter from Eliza Julia's brother-in-law, Hugh Ronalds, to George's brother Edward:

Your brother and Miss Wright have been upon the spot [Nashoba] for some time and George had been staying here for a few days only when he was unexpectedly obliged to return and in so doing was suddenly taken ill at Flim's ferry about 18 miles below Shawnee—I am unable to describe for you the cruelty and barbarity he experienced from those people—fortunately he had just discovered that Husbands, Fewkes and some others who had been sent down with a boatload bound for Memphis were detained near that place by adverse winds. Fewkes was sent up to let us know his situation. Mrs. George immediately set off in a dearborn—travelled all night—was overturned and hurt—arrived at the ferry unable to walk without assistance—she found George in a cabin quite alone. (Husbands having gone for Doctor) without food of any kind—covered with dirt—sitting up on a pallet upon the ground gnawing his fingers ends—he did not recognize her—she gave him some wine and by slow degrees he became sensible—he afterwards told her that he had been unable to get any assistance from the family except indeed that once having some beans crawled out into the porch he was literally turned over by the hogs and he expected they would begin to eat him. He then made a great effort and called loudly for assistance when one of the negroes of whom there were several was sent to run them off. Spring [Dr. Spring from Albion] not being at home when the news arrived did not get there so soon as Mrs. George and when arrived was taken so ill as to be laid up for some time. Posey from Shawnee arrived soon after and attended to both patients and strange to tell was himself soon after taken ill and was doctored by Spring. Ford, the keeper of the next ferry, hearing of their distress for they were still unable to get anything like accommodations from the family, sent his boat to fetch them down and they received at his house as much hospitality and kindness as had been wanting at Flims—George after a severe and dangerous illness got to Shawnee where he waited whilst Mrs. George came up here settled her business packed up and took her family down to Shawnee in company with Miss Camilla Wright (who had been staying with her during her sister's absence) at Memphis—Not being able to get passage in a steamboat they are all gone together in a flatboat and are probably by this time near their place of destination.[3]

After George's convalescence at Shawneetown, Eliza Julia closed Prairie House, gathered up her children and her guest, Camilla Wright, who had been left with her since fall, and with George set out for Nashoba.

Celia Morris Eckhardt, biographer of Fanny Wright, creates a love story between Fanny and George that cannot be corroborated. There is no doubt that Fanny Wright was dazzling. Martha, George's sister, wrote in 1825 to her brother in England,

> You will perhaps have heard of my Father's and George's trip to the East We are expecting their return next week with the Misses Wright who perhaps you may have heard of—they have been traveling with LaFayette and visited us a few months since most agreeable intelligent *real ladies* the eldest is considerably taller than my brother and are both women of amicable mind and manner.[4]

Not only was Fanny attractive, but her intelligent and liberal ideas made her a sought-after conversationalist, speaker, and writer. Her life is marked by her conquests of one gentleman after another who, attracted by her vivacity and personal charm, assisted her in her projects. Given her writing and speeches about the tyrannies of marriage, the associations she had with men were described by some of her critical contemporaries as evidence of her belief in free love. Oddly, Fanny's relationships with LaFayette, Robert Dale Owen, and others with whom she spent even more time than she did with George Flower are asserted by Eckhardt to have been "safely platonic."[5]

In Elliott's *Robert Dale Owen's Travel Journal*, Robert Dale Owen protests to his sister, Anne, "—I am no more likely to fall in love (as it is called) with her [Fanny Wright] than with yourself—"[6] so perhaps Fanny and Robert Dale *were* only platonic friends.

Perkins and Wolfson, early biographers of Fanny Wright, wrote that

> One has already several instances of Fanny's ability to attract and retain in her service as long as she needed them those she recognized as kindred souls. In the case of George Flower, however, one must admit that she had come upon him at a moment when he was especially vulnerable to her kind of appeal.[7]

It is notable that Perkins and Wolfson conclude "that the union of interests which resulted in this case, was as short-lived as it was sudden."[8]

In 1939, when they were writing, perhaps it was not so common to jump to the conclusion that friends became lovers. Eckhardt, however, has picked up some of the words from Perkins and Wolfson and has carried the idea beyond verification. In Eckhardt's view, "At the same time he [George] was so vulnerable to women that his sexuality had disrupted and marked his life."[9]

Perkins and Wolfson's mention of George's vulnerability, which Eckhardt picks up, refers to the fact that George had had a failed marriage in England and started life anew with Eliza Julia in Indiana and Illinois.

George had married his cousin, Jane Dawson, the daughter of Richard Flower's sister, about 1807. The marriage was not a happy one. The couple separated and lived apart after 1815. There were three sons born to the union: Henry, who died in England as an infant, George, and Richard, who came to America with their father. George and Jane had lived apart in England for several years before George went to America. George and Eliza Julia were married, bigamously as they both knew, in 1817 and had lived and worked together for nine years when the Wrights arrived in Albion. It did not seem to matter to either Eliza Julia or George that he had been married when he left England. In his account of this story, Faux wrote, "having missed his chance of happiness in his first, he was determined to try a second marriage which promised better things."[10]

George and Jane Dawson Flower were finally divorced on 15 January 1836.[11] He and Eliza Julia were remarried on 18 March 1836 in the Edwards County Court by Judge Harlan. Jane Dawson Flower did come to the United States later for the wedding of her son George, but she only went as far west as Pittsburgh. Although there can be no doubt that Fanny spent a great deal of Flower money, both Richard's and George's, on Nashoba and commanded much of George's time and attention, there is nothing to support the theory that this relationship was not also "safely platonic." One may doubt that George's vulnerability, if it ever existed, lasted until 1826, when Eckhardt claims he and Fanny became lovers.

A related problem with Eckhardt's construction of a love story is that it is extended to diminish Eliza Julia, who is described by Eckhardt as the cause of George Flower's leaving Nashoba and thereby causing its failure. Eckhardt wrote of Eliza Julia,

Eliza Flower was nursing a baby and keeping track of two small children. Even had she believed in Nashoba, she could have taken no part in the work that drew the rest of them together. She was bound to resent being peripheral to the central purpose there, and perhaps it was her resentment that prompted the Flowers to settle in Memphis.[12]

It may well have been good judgment, not resentment, that caused Eliza Julia to want to live in Memphis. She had lost her first baby in the early days of Albion when they lived in a rough, raw log cabin, and she undoubtedly saw no reason to repeat that tragedy and those hardships, particularly while she was caring for another recently born baby.

In the beginning of their acquaintance, the Wrights found much to admire in Eliza Julia. As in Fanny Wright's letter to Madame de Lasteyrie,[13] in which she extols Eliza Julia, so Camilla's letters to her friends, the Garnetts,[14] describe Eliza Julia as a charming and most intelligent woman; and of George and Eliza Julia, Camilla wrote, "Never I believe were two hearts more united." Fanny Wright wrote to Madame Charles de Lasteyrie,

I found Mr. Flower surrounded by a charming family, married to a woman endowed with the rarest qualities, working night and day in the cause of the negro. —His wife, a charming and most intelligent person, who has devoted herself day and night in the defense of the blacks, has arranged everything exactly right.[15]

Camilla's letter of 10 January 1826 to Julia Garnett, which recounts the story of George and Eliza Julia's bigamous marriage, describes both of them:

You will doubtless hear if you have not already heard all that the ill-natured malice of a misjudging world can suggest regarding

our association with Mr. George Flower & his wife for the
prosecution of this plan wh he has had for years at heart but wh
he cd not undertake without such pecuniary aid as we can supply
while on the other hand *we* cd as little have attempted [it] without
all the appliances & means to boot wh he has it in his power to
furnish, not to speak of his personal services, *wh I esteem as beyond
price*—He is moreover one of the most amiable beings I have ever
known & possesses all the qualifications that go to form an
agreeable & intelligent companion—

Respecting his marriage the only sin his worst enemy cd ever
bring to his charge *we are perfectly satisfied* there was no
circumstance attending it that cd shock the most scrupulous
morality—if not legally separated from his first wife (an odious
woman, his first cousin whom he was *entrapped* to marry at the
age of nineteen) divorce being obtained according to the English
law for but one cause, *adultery* & that being almost the only
charge he cd not have proved against her, they were only
separated by *mutual* consent she in writing & in the presence of
accredited witnesses, resign(ed)[ing] all claim over him as her
husband while he settled upon her every farthing of property she
had brought him on their ill starred marriage wh secured her an
ample independence.[16] . . .

The persecutions they [George and Eliza Julia] have in every
way endured it wd weary you to tell, but she possessed a spirit
that cd bear up under all her enemies cd devise, & as she has
often said to me—"our domestic felicity their malice cd never
interrupt & notwithstanding all we have endured I have enjoyed
years of happiness that my worst enemy might envy me"—I have
now had ample opportunity of seeing & judging the character of
this admirable woman who possesses one of the most noble,
*generous, and candid minds I have ever known in life—Her affections are
entirely centered in* her husband and her children & while I admire
& esteem her as my friend I do not & shall never feel for her that
*species of affection wh constitutes real friendship—We understand each
other* perfectly & I believe the person in the world next to her
husband she confides in most, is myself & she is so frank, so
open, so candid in her disposition & intercourse, I often tell her
that come what will there can never be a misunderstanding or
concealment between her and me. . . . This is the *guilty pair* with
whom we are *mainly* associated for the trial of the experiment in
the success of wh by the way she has not the least faith, but
whatever her husband wishes is her pleasure & happiness & once
engaged in she will help it forward more than any other
individual concerned in it.[17]

Camilla's assertion that Eliza Julia possessed one of the most noble, generous, and candid minds she had ever known in life was later reversed.

Camilla had been a houseguest of Eliza Julia and the elder Flowers from early fall 1825 until February 1826 when she traveled with George, Eliza Julia, and their children to Memphis, and as she wrote, she was a friend to Eliza Julia. The Flowers did work to make Nashoba thrive even while Fanny and Camilla went to New Harmony during the summer of 1826. In her letter of 12 November 1826 to Julia Garnett, Camilla, noting that the Flowers were visiting in Albion, anticipated that the Flowers would leave Nashoba.

Mr & Mrs Flower are absent on a visit to Illinois & as the old gentleman [Richard] talks of returning to Engd it is most probable his son will find himself obliged to return to his home to superintend their united property. in wh case we shall lose them as assistants in our undertaking.[18]

The Flowers did leave in October 1826 for a visit in Albion and did not return.

Camilla's devotion to her sister left no generosity for anyone who did not support Fanny. Despite her earlier assertion that "there can never be a misunderstanding or concealment between her & me," Camilla wrote on 8 December 1826,

He [George Flower] is a very amiable man & his society a great loss, for as I mentioned in my last they left this some weeks since on a visit to their home, from whence there is little probability of their return here owing to the proposed return, of the father, to Europe. Our anticipations with regard to his wife have not been so fully realized—she [Eliza Julia] is not in any way suited to fill any station in this establishment nor does she possess a mind calculated to enter into the views connected with it.[19]

Although caustic about her lack of enthusiasm for the Nashoba project, Camilla did not write that Eliza Julia was the cause of the Flowers' departure. To add to the impression that the failure of Nashoba was due to Eliza Julia's taking George away, Eckhardt quotes Frances Trollope, an English

writer and friend of Fanny Wright, who wrote Harriet
Garnett, 7 December 1828, of her visit to Nashoba in January
1828, "The jealousy of the wife made it impossible for [Fanny
Wright and George Flower] to continue together."[20] Trollope's
views were written nearly two years after the Flowers left
Nashoba. In the book that brought her great attention, Mrs.
Trollope wrote,

I do not exactly know what was the immediate cause which
induced Miss Wright to abandon a scheme which had taken such
possession of her imagination, and on which she expended so
much money; but many months had not elapsed before I learned,
with much pleasure, that she and her sister had also left it. I
think it probable that she became aware, upon returning to
Nashoba, that the climate was too hostile to their health.[21]

In summing up the failure of Nashoba, Waterman, a biographer of Frances Wright, offers at least five reasons why
Nashoba did not succeed, but none involves Eliza Julia.

If Eliza Julia truly was involved in a struggle with Fanny
to keep her husband, she was a formidable adversary. Like
Fanny Wright, Eliza Julia had strength of mind and the
courage of her convictions. While still a young woman in England, she had demonstrated that she, too, was a daring
woman for her age and class. She had a passionate interest in
politics. When Eliza Julia was in her late teens she had cut her
hair and donned her brother's military uniform in order that
she might be admitted to the Strangers' Gallery of the House
of Commons, where she wanted to hear the Charles James
Fox debates.[22] She did not accept the commonly held belief
that listening to a parliamentary debate was considered much
too taxing for a woman's delicate brain. An excellent horsewoman, she dared to insist on driving her own team, something few women of her time did.

There is no evidence that George was ever in love with
Fanny Wright or any woman other than Eliza Julia. Whether
one accepts Eckhardt's assertion that George and Fanny were
lovers, or a less romantic view that George's relationship with
Fanny was as safely platonic as Fanny's with Robert Dale
Owen, the return of the Flower family to Albion seems to in-
dicate that Eliza Julia won in the struggle for George Flower's
attention, affection, and dedication.

Party on Horseback Leaving Park House for a Ride on the English Prairie, May 1826, by Charles Alexandre LeSueur, courtesy of Muséum d'Histoire Naturelle du Havre

After George Flower described some of his anti-slavery work in his *History,* particularly his project of sending free blacks to Haiti, he wrote, "Thus ends the black chapter of our history." The Nashoba experiment might also be seen as black because it was another attempt to ameliorate the lives of blacks, because it failed, because George nearly lost his life in the effort, and because Eliza Julia had to leave her much-loved home in the English Settlement for a temporary residence in Memphis near Nashoba.

Seven years later, when Eliza Julia wrote to John, perhaps the memories of the women who came to dinner were not completely erased from her mind; they may account for some of the caution she expressed in her letter to her nephew. Clear to the reader of this first letter are her enthusiasm, her devotion to her family, and her appreciation of her husband. These same characteristics are more and more apparent in her subsequent letters to her nephew.

Chapter 2

"This is the Country for a poor labouring Man with a large Family."

Eliza Julia Flower

L IFE ON THE FRONTIER, or in the backwoods, as Eliza Julia called it, was an egalitarian experience, the major dynamic being that everyone worked. Although there were some few who would work as domestic help and as farm laborers, there was no servant class as there had been in England, with the result that physical labor was well known to all.

Eliza Julia seemed to thrive in this environment. When she began this correspondence with John in 1833, she was the mother of five living children. She might no longer have been the outstanding beauty she was at twenty-five, but she still retained the qualities attributed to her by William Faux, an early visitor to the English Settlement who wrote when describing George Flower,

> His lady seems the happiest and most elegant female I have
> seen, and perfectly suited to her present or any situation being
> neither above the cottage nor below the palace. . . . Well indeed
> might four gentlemen contend for the prize! The gay, graceful,
> modest, hearty, anticipating kindness of this lady makes every
> guest feel himself at home and loth to depart.[1]

At this time, the Flowers lived comfortably in Prairie House, which Faux described as "the completest log cabin I have ever seen, near his father. It contains six or seven rooms with other useful buildings, and as a log establishment I will venture to say, possesses more comfort and elegance than any ever seen in America."[2]

Prairie House was only seventy yards from Park House, the home of George's parents, Richard and Elizabeth Fordham Flower. When Richard Flower first came to the English Prairie he built, in addition to his home, both a grist mill and a cotton gin in Albion, as he said, "for the good of the settlement." He later added a pottery works and kiln and constructed a rope walk at Park House. Richard Flower died on 2 September 1829, leaving his widow to occupy Park House alone. George's brother William had also died, and his younger brother, Edward, had returned to live out his life in England. Thus by 1833, when the correspondence began, George was responsible for managing the entire Flower agricultural estate, which was extensive, for his mother, Elizabeth. He knew that as eldest son he would inherit Park House upon her death.

Because even the poorest of immigrants could in a short time earn enough money to buy cheap government land and thereafter become landowners themselves, keeping laborers was always a severe problem for the more affluent Englishmen who had more land than they could manage alone. Englishmen like the Flowers were accustomed to being able to hire servants in England. In Illinois and on other parts of the frontier, few persons worked for others. The shortage of servants existed partly because people were absorbed in working their own farms and shops, but also because Americans were imbued with a spirit of independence, a feeling of equality that made it difficult for them to accept a second-class position. There was no lower class whose members understood that their place was to be in service. On the American frontier, with the exception of slaves and indentured servants, everyone was free to work for himself. From the beginning, the Flowers were almost chronically short of laborers. Since before 1833, some of their estate fields had lain idle for want of workers, they had begun to practice owner-tenant farming, that is, farming on shares. The agreement was usually ten bushels of grain to the landowner for each acre farmed. The historian James Madison makes the point that without a family to do the work, the frontiersman was unable to be more than a hunter.[3] Since the Flower family was no different in this respect, everyone in the family was obliged to work. Therefore, when Eliza Julia wrote to John on 11 March 1833 that she might accept his brother, she wanted it understood that he, like every other member of the family, would have to work with his hands and work hard and—although certain of food and lodging—would not have much cash.

While Eliza Julia was emphasizing the realities of life in the backwoods, she did admit that "this is better than any place on earth," and many happinesses fill family recollections of those early days. One example of those family memories was written in 1942 by Eliza Julia's great-granddaughter, recalled from stories she had heard from her grandmother.

When we were children we used to beg our mother to tell us the story of her mother, when she was a child on the Illinois Prairie. This grandmother of ours, whom we knew only from the photograph of a very erect woman with her hair held back from her forehead by a snood, was one of the children of George Flower, who had founded the English Settlement at Albion, Illinois. There were eight of these children—four boys and four girls—and when we were small the story we liked most to hear was how, on fine days in spring and summer, they were permitted to shepherd the thousand Merino sheep whose strain my great-great-grandfather had brought over from England.

They took their dinner, their books and slates, and pencils and on horseback with their dogs and the sheep, went several miles away from their home to where a small log playhouse and a shelter for the horses had been built on a hill overlooking the prairie. . . . First we wanted to hear for the thousandth time just how the prairie looked: that it was not simply miles of treeless land, but rolling stretches and slopes, with groves of enormous oak trees, as in an English park. In April it became smooth and green as a well cared for lawn. In May the surrounding woods grew darker green. With June the grass intensified in brilliance, and millions of flowers—very tiny and immensely big—blossomed through it. At noon when the sun was high and hot, the sheep would crowd under the shade of the oak trees, and after their picnic dinner the boys and girls would fall asleep in their playhouse.[4]

Either memory dims over the generations or Eliza Julia was also a superb psychologist to be able to turn a sheep fold into a playhouse and a serious job into a picnic.

There was a great curiosity in Europe and in England, as well as on the East Coast of the United States, about the dimensions of everyday living on the frontier. Letters from the backwoods, like these of Eliza Julia, are full of details about the costs and availability of food and opportunities for employment. Eliza Julia's letter of 11 March 1833 reports those dimensions specifically, with special emphasis on the roles of the members of the family.

March 11, 1833

Near Albion Illinois

My dear John,

I am quite concerned that unavoidable circumstances together with indisposition has prevented me from answering your very welcome Letter before—I have been considering over and over again in my own mind what I could do for Charles—First I thought I would invite him to come and live with us—as my own son and work with us and be in all respects provided for by us— again I thought that wouldn't do—The habits of Young Men from Europe especially from England are so different from ours that it is almost impossible for them to be satisfied with our mode of Life—You who have been brought up to *one* business in a regular way have no idea of our numerous avocations—We (both Men and Women)—are obliged to put our hands to whatever work is required to be done no matter how important or how menial, for instance—We having a large family are sometimes without any female servant for six months together—consequently I Cook, Clean, Wash, Recieve Company, Nurse my Children, Visit,—do all that comes to hand as a matter of course, again I get a good servant and then I rest a little—Our Eldest Girl Emma 14 years old milks the Cows, feeds the pet lambs—learns her daily Lessons— makes her own clothes—rides on Horse back, bridles and Saddles her own Horse—Collects the Eggs—raises the Poultry, dances well,—makes Pies Puddings Bread etc—Alfred our Eldest Boy 11 years old is sole shepard of our flock of sheep consisting of 4 or 5 hundred, feeds them night and morning takes them out in the Prairie to graze—brings them home to fold in the Evening, gets his lessons between times Chops Wood, Gardens, feeds the Pigs, and after Supper amuses himself in reading writing, drawing or what else he pleases The Younger Children assist the Elder ones or their Father or me,—and never think they are to be idle when we desire them to work—Mr. Flower is occupied fully in several different Business's—We have a large Farm upon wh. we live,—a Rope walk on the Farm—a Pottery in the Town of Albion 1 ½ miles from this place—also a Flour and Corn Mill, sometimes we board all the work hands—sometimes they board themselves— This Year we Farm upon Shares according to the Custom of the Country viz—the Master or Owner—finds Land, Horses, Implements, Seed—and the other party finds all the Labour and after harvest—each takes Half—a Good Working hand upon a farm gets 50 cts per day and in harvest time from 62 to 75 cts per day—a Mechanic earns more a Carpenter Wheelwright Brick Layer etc etc. from 75 to $1 per day—our Miller gets 62 ½ our Potter and Ropemaker something more—Our Settlement is small tho thriving—but we are quite a plain people and works of art, skill, and fancy are quite out of our way at present—I mention all these things to shew you that Charles wouldn't with old Country habits be likely to be happy or useful here and if he could fall in with any Trade with or near you it would be more likely to benifit You don't tell me what work he has ever done what *kind* I mean— Whether he has ever learn'd any trade—or what he most inclines to—You must tell me all about him in your next—if he was competent to keep a Boy and Girls School—there would be a good opening here—and if he was attentive we could almost assure him success. I wish very much we could do something for him, but I dare not at a venture invite him to come 1000 miles without I knew that it would be mutually benificial—I am rejoiced that you appear to be so happy—and so determined to be independant always preserve that spirit—and you will be almost sure to succeed—I am glad that you have married an American Lass—depend on it they make by far the best Wives for this Country—and since you have been so fortunate in getting a kind affectionate Girl who loves [you] dearly—always love and cherish her, as the best treasure you can possess and always be a Lover and never fancy that a crime which makes the happiness of your Life—Give my love to her for your sake and as I hope some day to see you both have no doubt but I shall love her for her own—Tell Charles to write to me as frankly as you have done and describe himself and his wishes and capabilities—as fully as he can, if we were near you I have no doubt but we could assist him much—

not with Money for we have so large a Family and this is such a trading Barter Country that we require all the Money we can make—but in some kind of business if he is industrious—we certainly would put him—You must write to me again it will always give me pleasure to hear all about yourself your Wife your little Son yr Brother Charles and Charles Wray—or any of you Youngsters who are fighting your way thro the World—I did not tell you that Living by that I mean food firing and House Rent are very cheap here—good boarding at $1.50—Beef 2cts Pork 3 Veal 3 Mutton 3-½ Venison the finest and fattest at $1 the whole deer— or 25 the 2 hams Butter 12-½—Eggs 6-½ per:doz.—fowls 8 cts—a good Cow from $10 to $12 Corn from 16 to 20 cts and plenty of all these things and good of their kind beautiful Honey 50 cts per Gall fine Turkey 12-½ and 25—Prairie fowls—(Grouse) 4 cts each in abundance Vegetables of all kinds in the highest perfection— This is the Country for a poor labouring Man with a large family—but it isn't at present the Country for the fine arts or for those who cannot labour—I like the back Woods as this is call'd better than any place upon Earth—I came into the country from Choice and I am a thorough American in principle and practice— We live in the same Cabins Log wh we built when we first came here 15 years ago—very humble in appearance but plaster'd and colour'd withinside with deep porches back and front good size'd rooms neat clean airy and cheerful—they stand on a fine meadow like a Park—Blue Grass up to door situated on a beautiful Prairie—good Wells and good Tanks—it is a lovely Country and remarkably healthy—Good night dear John—Give kind love to your little Circle—I am your affectionate Aunt

Eliza J. Flower

PS I percieve when reading your letter over again that Charles has been brought up in the Rugg making nothing of that kind is wanted here but do tell me if you think he would make a Farmer or Shepard or a Miller I mean to work with his own hands—just as a Labourer does in England for that is what we all do here— write directly and I will answer.

Cooperation among people on the frontier is legendary. When there was a house to raise, frontiersmen came to help, but as friendly neighbors and equal partners in the social event, not as hirelings. One English settler, John Woods, explained that while the Americans often shared labor, the English did not.

Woods wrote,

We did not make any frolic in husking our corn but did it ourselves; but the Americans seldom do anything without having one, thus, they have husking, reaping, rolling frolics, etc. etc. —among the females they have picking, sewing and quilting frolics.[5]

The English preferred to do their own work or hire farm laborers if they had the means. Only in rare circumstances, as in a barn raising or cabin raising, where greater physical strength than one man possessed was a necessity, would they call upon their neighbors for help, contributing to the stereotype held by some frontier people that the English were standoffish, perhaps too proud to ask for help, and perhaps considered themselves better than their neighbors.

Compounding the servant problem was antipathy still existing among some Americans toward the English immigrants, which lessened their desire to work for them. Although George Flower, writing in 1860 of the early days of the 1820s, said that he could recall little friction between the earliest settlers and the English immigrants, there were others who could. George, in his reveries, was suppressing the unpleasant. Some of the early American settlers had lost members of their families to Indian raids incited by the English during the War of 1812. George recalled that once, when Eliza Julia accompanied him on a visit to a respectable American farmer on Big Prairie, the farmer's wife left the cabin and went into the woods, refusing to come back until the visitors left. The farmer apologized to Mrs. Flower for his wife's disappearance by saying that she had lost a brother at the Battle of the River Raisin and would not meet an English person.[6] Memories of such traumatic events did not help the English to be accepted by the Americans.

Then too, real cultural differences existed in styles of living between the English and the Americans. The unlettered frontiersmen never really accepted the educated and mannered middle-class English. Americans were more likely to take one day at a time and seemed to lack the industrious-

ness and drive of the English men and women who were determined to tame the prairie.

The historian Alice Felt Tyler wrote of these differences,

The conquest of the wilderness was an arduous task, exacting and
monotonous and burdensome. It was wasteful of human life,
especially of women and children, and it was destructive of
culture and neglectful of social relationships. The frontiersman
was repelled by pretension, preferring his acquaintances to be no
better than himself. An educated Englishman, residing in Illinois
in the 1820s commented bitterly on this trait: "A man to be
popular in our new western towns and with the country folk
around, should be acquainted with everybody, shake hands with
everybody, and wear an old coat, with at least one good hole in it.
A little whiskey and a few squirts of tobacco juice are
indispensable. From the former you may be excused if you treat
liberally to others. If there is one fellow a little more greasy and
dirty than another, be sure to hug him. Do all this and you have
done much to being a popular man."[7]

George Flower was that "educated Englishman residing
in Illinois" quoted by Tyler, and he wrote at this time with
deserved bitterness. His son had been murdered, for no apparent reason, by a frontiersman named Meredith, and the
murderer was freed by a jury of his peers although it was
common knowledge that he was guilty.[8] Before his son's
death, George truly believed he had the ability to get along
well with all Americans, from Thomas Jefferson to Capt.
Burke, hunter and woodsman. In writing to his sister while
on his first exploratory journey of America in 1816, he
described an English traveler in America and said, "I hear of
H's fame everywhere I go as a Jno. Bull, but as for me I am so
accomplished that I am taken for a true Yankee."[9]

The air of equality and independence among the Americans was quickly acquired by the recently arrived English.
Eliza Julia's father-in-law, Richard Flower, who was no
egalitarian, liked to tell the story of Biddy. A gentleman hired
a female servant who insisted as a condition of employment
on sitting down at the dinner table with the family; the condition was consented to and then a project for a cure was
planned. A party was invited to dinner and Biddy took her

place at the table. When she wanted anything, a gentleman arose and offered it to Biddy. Biddy was asked to drink a glass of wine first by one of the gentlemen and then another. Biddy was urged not to trouble herself about anything and was so ceremoniously treated that she felt awkward in the company of the guests. The next day she said to her mistress, "Madam, I had rather give up dining at your table."[10]

Eliza Julia, who was after all a generation younger than her father-in-law and a more flexible person, almost immediately accepted the American custom of eating with her servants, unless the Flowers had guests. James Stuart, an English traveler who visited the English Settlement in 1833, noted,

Mr. and Mrs. Flower are obliged to adopt the custom which is quite universal here—of eating with their servants who are quite numerous; they all eat and drink alike, but Mr. Flower makes it a condition, in hiring servants, that when strangers come to see them, they live apart from the servants.[11]

Stuart was probably writing of "hired hands" and male farm servants, who were always more numerous than house servants, and since he was writing nearly fourteen years after Richard Flower described Biddy's cure, one can assume that more and more the servants became part of the family.

Critics of the English Settlement used the labor shortage to discourage others from going to Illinois during the first days of the settlement and complained that it was impossible to find servants there. Richard Flower disagreed.

It has been reported that we can get no servants. This is true in a degree, because the price of services is such, as soon to elevate to a state of independence: but I have found no want of persons to work for hire, even in domestic situations; those that are wanted most are farming laborers; good ploughmen are in request and can obtain 12 dollars per month and their board. Female servants from eight to ten dollars according to their respective merits; these are in great request; and what perhaps is to them still more pleasing, their industry is the certain road to marriage. Our young females are almost all engaged in this way, and we certainly lose good servants, but have the pleasure of seeing them well settled.[12]

In her third letter, 23 March 1833, Eliza Julia enlarged her description of her family and some aspects of their life together as she tried again to make it clear to John that life in Illinois was not like living in England or in New York. As she had done before, in this letter too, she unabashedly spoke of her love for her husband, his love for her, and her devotion to her home.

Persons who write about the women who lived in early America describe the lives of frontier women to be lonely, with few contacts outside their own families. Within their homes they are described as living in subordinate roles to their husbands, who dominated everything. By contrast, the modern American family is said to emerge at the beginning of the nineteenth century, and its features include mutual respect and love between husbands and wives, specialized roles for women such as educating and disciplining children, and an important voice for women in the total affairs of the family. In the modern family, no longer are all decisions made by the patriarch. Eliza Julia, living on the Illinois frontier in the 1830s, is more like the women described in modern families than those of the earlier type. Only in the number of children that she bore does she resemble the typical frontier woman. The distinction becomes clearer as we read each of her letters.

Sunday

March 23rd 1833
Near Albion

My dear John,

I wrote you by last mail but Mr. Flower wasn't satisfied with my letter and therefore I write again, I would like very much to have Charles with us—if I thought he could turn his hand to any thing as my Children do—without feeling it a disgrace to work— or disagreable so to do—and then after a time if Mr. Flower and he were satisfied with each other Mr. F. would put him into some business—or give him wages—if he had been on a farm and could take that department from Mr. F. I should be thankful—if he understood Milling or a Saw Mill we have a vacant place, but John the truth to tell ye—I have been so plagued with young men from England sent to us—to cure them of their City habits—and to

make farmers of them etc—and then after doing all in our power
they have turn'd out so troublesome that I have said I never
would venture upon an Old Country Youth again—and then if I
was to invite my *relation* and he and Mr. Flower did not agree that
would mortify me beyond all things Mr. Flower is the mildest and
best of Human beings, his heart is all benevolence and kindness—
He was very much pleased with your letter and said directly—
"invite your nephew down to live with us" my heart said the
same—but I determined to consider consequences and I chose to
speak just as freely to you as if you were my own Sons—and if
you were here I should in all things treat you as such—I have
been kindly and handsomely treated by all my Husband's
Relations—ever since I married—my Relations have never treated
him with common civility—of them therefore I do not wish to
hear—but of you young ones—I *do* like to hear and should like to
befriend—our family consists of My Husband and myself 7
children 3 girls and 4 Boys—Generally three or 4 Visitors
sometimes 2 or 3 Servants sometimes none at all, Our House is
always comfortable and respectable our Meals and Hours of rising
and going to bed regular—Our Children are at present very
promising (tho there is no saying how any of them will turn
out)—Mr. F. and I have been I think I may say uncommonly
happy—and I am not at all ashamed to say that at the age of 40—I
am more in love with him than I was when I married and so I
believe is he with me, we have always studied each others
happiness in every particular however small—and it has brought
us our reward, With these feelings towards my Husband you
must not wonder that I am cautious how I invite one of my own
relatives to reside with us—knowing as I do how one individual
may either mar or contribute to the comfort of the whole family
for myself I am tolerably determin'd and high spirited. My Home
my family are my idols—and if I saw anything going on which I
disapproved of in any one of its members I should instantly
speak—nor should I rest till all was set right again This has always
been my rule, without any violence, and the consequences is that
not one of the Children or Servants ever think of contradicting
us—or refuse to do any thing that we require of them and we on
our part always study their comfort their tempers their tastes and
allow of every innocent enjoyment that we can command for them,
and this is the only way that I would live or would wish to live—
and upon this point as upon most others Mr. F. and I exactly agree.

Now my dear John if after all I have said Charles would like to
come and you would like him to come and he could find the

Portrait of George Flower, courtesy of the Patricia Flower Martin
Collection

means to get down here we shall be very glad to see him and I
will supply him with Cloaths etc. and everything else that he
wants, if he is a good boy and respectable in his conduct he shall
want for nothing that my own Children enjoy and my Children
will all hail him immediately as a Cousin or a brother—His Uncle
will say little and do much for him, My own Kindred have never
been seen in this Country—You may suppose that I should wish
his first impression to be favourable—and his future good conduct
to keep up and increase that first impression—He need bring but
one change of Cloaths—and I will immediately furnish his
wardrobe according to the fashion of this Country—I have plenty
of everything around me but *portable dollar*—of them Mr. F.
requires all in business

Sunday April 1st—I have been thinking my dear John—how
Charles could get down here at a small expense—I'll tell what a
Young Man did who came last summer—He had a small sum of
money which he did not wish to touch till he reached us—he
therefore with ten dollars wh he had besides purchased of a
Wholesale Jeweller in New York ten dollars worth of Jewellary—
big rings, Chains Waist Buckles, Broaches, Pins, Lockets, etc. all of
the cheapest kind of course—these he sold on the road at a very
high percentage—and absolutely found his way down to us—
without touching his *little capital*—I mention this because as you
are in that line perhaps you could get these things for him better
than money—What do you intend to do if you leave your present
employer this spring? I wish you were a Farmer. I would offer you
and your wife—(she being of this Country and not afraid to
work)—a nice snug farm directly with flock of the best and most
approved kind—I wish you co'd send some good straping farmers
here who would rent our land at the customary price of so many
Bushels per acre. We have a quantity of beautiful Land but Mr.
Flower and I are growing old, and I do not wish to extend our
present business's—but I should like the Land to be Rented out
and put into cultivation for a few years when our Children will be
old enough to farm for themselves. How I wish dear boy that I
could chat with you—I could tell you more in one hour than I can
write in one week—I want to *look* at you—I am sorry you have got
that awful Andrews *Nose and Wiskers*—I was in hopes you had
taken your Mothers face for a Pattern instead of your fathers!—but
either way I should like to see you! had not you a brother William
and where is he? and where is Charles Wray?—do you know
anything about *Wool*? We have a large flock of Saxony and Merino

sheep but we can not find a suitable market for the Wool this side the Mountains—I shall always pay the Postage of my letters to you but I desire you not to pay your letters to me—and I shall always be glad to hear from you whenever you like to write—My kind love to your Wife and Boy and Charles and C WRAY—I thank you for the newspaper you sent—dont fancy that newspapers either frighten or offend me—I am sorry only when they mislead the reader—you see I am a Jewess—I like to be one quite as well as a Gentile!—Goodbye dear John, I am

Your affectionate Aunt

Eliza J. Flower

In these two letters, Eliza Julia begins to describe the life of the Flower family in detail. Particularly interesting are her references to her personal values. When she writes that she is not ashamed to say that at age forty "I am more in love with him than when I married," she makes a more personal statement than one usually finds from women of her time and place. When she states, "My home, my family are my idols," she reveals that her devotion to them is another important part of her character. In her offer to John to pay all the postage for correspondence between them one can see her generosity. As she describes the way a person traveling to the west might defray some of his expenses, she shows her good business sense. Eliza Julia's statement that she is a Jewess refers to her Andrews family blood line, not to religious belief. Her grandfather, father, and brother were all well-educated protestant Congregational clergymen. Among all the persons who visited and later wrote about the English Prairie, only one ever mentioned Eliza Julia as Jewish. Perhaps her reference to her ancestry was in reply to something in the article on Albion and his aunt which John Andrews had read in New York.

The conditions of living changed slowly on the frontier. Fred Gustorf, who came to Illinois in 1834, wrote describing the life of a farmer near Albion in terms that closely resemble Eliza Julia's admonitions written to her nephew, John:

The occupation of farming is almost impossible for an immigrant in this country, especially one who is physically unfit for this kind of work and therefore dependent upon others for help. He would be foolhardy, because it would lead to nothing in the long run, as experience has demonstrated in many cases.

During the harvest season I worked for a farmer without pay. For this purpose I had made for myself several sets of working clothes out of rough linen, and mingled with laborers in the hayfields. In the beginning I worked only two hours daily, one hour in the morning and one in the afternoon. I did the easiest work: raking hay. Easy as the work was, the burning sun was intolerable. The thermometer rose to 100 and over. After an hour's work I was completely soaked with perspiration. I had to change my clothes several times daily.

Other kinds of work which I was able to do were turning the swath with a wooden fork, stacking it when it was dry, piling up the hay, loading it on the wagon, then unloading the wagon onto the haystacks. Stacking the hay with an iron fork is very tiring, and even if one works without a shirt and drinks water constantly, it is almost unbearable. These jobs are nothing compared with mowing, plowing, thinning Indian corn, and grubbing; also stacking oats in stubby fields. It is almost impossible for someone who is not used to this kind of work from his youth to handle the scythe, the plow, and the axe to advantage. Americans know best how to swing the axe.—

Whoever wants to be a farmer in the western states and is unable to do the hard work himself has to hire laborers with money and good words, which is always difficult and sometimes impossible. Among one hundred laborers you might find one whose work is satisfactory. A farmer who can not do the work himself must have at least one hired man at a cost of $120 to $170 per year. The main problem is at harvest time when help is hard to find. The average daily wage is a dollar to a dollar and a half per day plus board. Since help is so hard to find, the American farmers help each other in building their log houses. Prices of farm products are low compared to the cost of farming.

A farmer's life is neither romantic nor idyllic—just hard work with small rewards. A person who has not tried it has no idea what problems are involved.[13]

Later, in January 1842, William Dobell, an Englishman who came to Albion to be a teacher, described life in the town. In a letter to his sister, he included his suggestions for a young farmer who might come to this pleasant place to make his living. Dobell's ideas sound similar to Eliza Julia's accounts of the costs of food and the prices that might be obtained from the sale of produce, and also similar to Gustorf's account written ten years earlier. Dobell warns,

It is a mistaken notion in England, that a little labour is *here* sufficient for the means of subsistence. Constant labour & economy are necessary in every occupation to ensure desirable success here as well as elsewhere and it is useless for persons to emigrate to this Country unless they possess property sufficient to maintain themselves, or are of decidedly industrious and persevering habits.[14]

In his book *Errors of Immigrants*, published a year before Dobell's letter, George Flower did not hesitate to specify who bore the burden.

The circumstances of the country are such as to make labour fall more constantly upon the woman than upon the man. The family meals are to be prepared every day, the washing, the cleaning, the bed-making, the scouring, must be carried on, perhaps when all hired help has left, an occurrence not unfrequent. Let none deceive themselves with the fallacious idea, that by good management and judicious arrangement they can escape bona fide hard work. Good management will necessarily do much to alleviate the female task, but it will not do all. In the toils incident to a large family, there are times and seasons under the best management, when all the nerve and sinew that a woman can muster, must be put in actual requisition. If my country women cannot consent to exchange useless habits of feebleness falsely called gentility, never let them think of coming to Illinois. If their good sense prevails, and they resolutely undertake what is necessary to be done, with cheerfulness and good will, they will find kind neighbors to teach and assist them, and what is yet better, they will be their own best friends. Great is their reward; for females of delicate constitution, poor health, and tender spirits, can attain to strong health and cheerfulness, by their change of country, and habits of life—One of the greatest of evils that can befall a man in his emigration, is the discontent (when it does occur) of the females of his family.[15]

George could well have taken Eliza Julia as his model for this statement. She had exchanged a life of ease in England for every menial chore of the frontier; she turned her hand to every kind of duty without complaint and almost always with cheerfulness and good will. George may not have fully appreciated how unusual his wife was even though he recognized that not all women on the frontier measured up to her standards.

As Eliza Julia wrote in her second letter, 23 March 1823, George, with his background of limitless hospitality at his parents' Marden Hill, and later at Park House, was ready at once to have Charles Andrews come to live with them. Eliza Julia, who accepted the decision, was perhaps more cautious because her relatives were not kind to George, as she wrote, they "have never treated him with common civility." The coolness or unkindness may have been because of the bigamous marriage. However, in her letters of March 1833, Eliza Julia's main concern was that Charles had to understand that life on the frontier was hard: although it had many rewards, she and her large family all labored as though they too were servants. There were few other options for those who had invested most of their capital in land. Charles would have to join the family in working hard.

Chapter 3

"[The Ohio River is] the grand thoroughfare to all the Western States."

George Flower

T HE ROUTE TO THE ENGLISH PRAIRIE had not changed very much by 1833 from that taken by most of the English on their way to Albion and Wanborough in 1817. Eliza Julia advised John about the best way to come to Illinois in her next letter.

Near Albion

April 23, 1833

My dear John,

I was from home when Yours of the 31st March arrived and am very sorry that the delay on my part in answering your Letters should have caused you any uneasiness, I hope however that ere this you have recieved my letters and I now write expressly to invite Charles to live with us—and to come immediately if you between you can raise the means of his conveyance to this place directly he arrives here we will provide for all his wants therefore he need be under no uneasiness upon that score—I presume that the cheapest and quickest mode of travelling will be by *Water* a great part of the way and when he arrives at *ShawneeTown* upon the *Ohio Illinois* a well known stopping place for all Steamboats— let him inquire for *Mr. Thomas Docker Tavern Keeper and Merchant* who is our Agent in that Town—and he will entertain Charles whilst there and find him a proper conveyance to our House where Charles will find a cordial welcome—Charles must not

59

expect at *first* any thing more than to be provided for with our own Children, and if after some time he makes himself valuable to us by his conduct—Mr. Flower will put him into some good and respectable Business and push him up in the world if it is not his own fault—I hope that you will then send for your brother George directly—and if you cannot do better for him in New York we will try and do something for him here—This invitation to Charles is sent under the supposition that you can find nothing for him to do in New York—but if anything should have arisen since your last letter wh promises Charles a living *upon no account let it slip,* but embrace it directly as the best thing that he can do for our mode of living is so different from a City Life that what we might call *good* you might be dissatisfied with—I say this because I have seen so many persons both young and old quite disappointed when they have come into this new Country, and I am always afraid of misleading any one on that point. I think however that I have said enough upon this head not to *mislead you* and therefore I will revert to other parts of your Letter—Poor William![1] —I remember him a pretty quiet little Boy! I have often wondered what became of him—I pity your poor Mother—hers has been a life of sorrow indeed! I hope it will be a comfort to her to hear that you Boys are provided for give my love to her when you write but do not send my letters out of your own hands to any one—I am glad to hear that Jemima is so happy and much very much should I like to see you and your Wife—and boy! I am glad you are in a good business and wish that your health was better—I have just been a trip on horseback of upwards of two hundred and fifty miles with my Husband upon the National Road in this State—There is a good opening there for a person with a small Capital—for a store—if anything should turn up there or anywhere [else] that we think would be beneficial to *you* we shall bear you in mind and write you of the same—If you should know of any good Labouring Hands Canal Diggers or road makers—men who are seeking employment—they would find good earnings upon the National Road in Illinois and you might direct them to Mr. Flower who would immediately direct them to the Contractors on that Road and who are good men to pay their hands—if they brought their own spades or fly tools they would get still higher wages—Good Night dear John—my time is gone is gone—We all unite in love to you all—write directly and tell me your decision about Charles—we will write to Mr. Docker by this Mail to inform him of the probability of Charles appearance there,—and whether he comes or not that will do no harm—I am in hopes that your next letter will bring me a few lines from Charles himself—

I am dear John

Yr affectionate Aunt

Eliza J. Flower

The best route to the West was still by water. Returning from his mission to England, George and Eliza Julia had made their second trip to Illinois by way of the Ohio River. Traveling with them were their month-old daughter, Emma, George's two sons by his first marriage, boys of six and eight, his brother, William, and his cousin, Maria Fordham. They purchased a keelboat for the family and a flatboat for the horses and carriage, lashed the two boats together, and hired four Englishmen for oarsmen. It was prudent to have an experienced pilot, but unfortunately for the Flowers the one they hired deserted them shortly after the trip began, and George was forced to take the steering oar himself. It was a hair-raising trip. In addition to going aground and having to pole the boats free, the party faced some very dangerous sections of the Ohio River, particularly one named Dead Man's Shoals. Travelers on the Ohio River during this time used a guide called the *Pittsburgh Navigator,* a book with maps of the river listing all the shoals, islands, and dangerous places. Using the navigation book, traveling by day and tying up at night, they proceeded successfully until they came to Dead Man's Shoals. The *Navigator* warned of a dangerous channel of rapid water to be avoided at all costs; it would be recognized by a certain island of great length close to the north shore. When the Flower boats approached this island they went aground, because George was unable to judge how far the sand bar extended from the point of the island into the river. While he poled off the bar, the current caught them and sent their boats into the exact channel they were to avoid. George described his feelings as follows:

I felt, as we approached the danger, as a man may be supposed to feel when he finds himself and craft drawing into the waters of

61

M, Weed THE

NAVIGATOR,

CONTAINING

DIRECTIONS FOR NAVIGATING

THE MONONGAHELA, ALLEGHENY,

OHIO AND MISSISSIPPI RIVERS;

WITH AN AMPLE

ACCOUNT OF THESE MUCH ADMIRED WATERS,

FROM THE HEAD OF THE FORMER

TO THE MOUTH OF THE LATTER;

AND A CONCISE

DESCRIPTION OF THEIR TOWNS, VILLAGES,

HARBORS, SETTLEMENTS, &c.

WITH MAPS OF THE OHIO AND MISSISSIPPI.

TO WHICH IS ADDED

AN APPENDIX,

CONTAINING

AN ACCOUNT OF LOUISIANA,

AND

OF THE MISSOURI AND COLUMBIA RIVERS,

AS DISCOVERED BY THE VOYAGE UNDER

CAPTS. LEWIS AND CLARK.

———

ELEVENTH EDITION.

———

PITTSBURGH:

PRINTED AND PUBLISHED BY CRAMER & SPEAR,

FRANKLIN HEAD, WOOD STREET.

1821.

Title page of *The Navigator Containing Directions for Navigating the Monongahela, Allegheny, Ohio and Mississippi Rivers*, 1821, Pittsburgh, Willard Library, Evansville, Indiana, courtesy of Special Collections, Willard Library

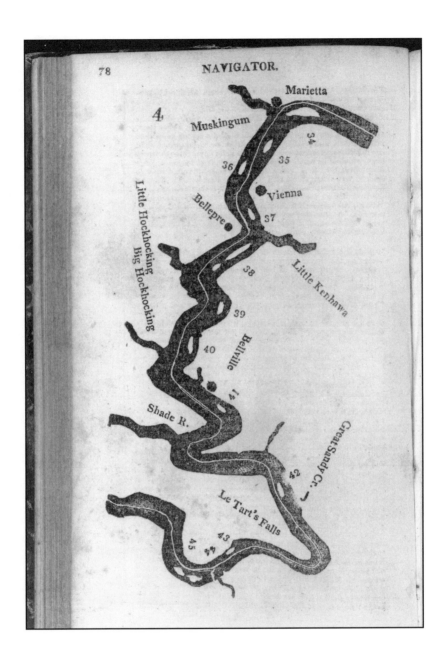

Illustrative map from *The Navigator,* courtesy of Special Collections, Willard Library

the Niagara, I was for a short time, uncertain, weak and helpless through fright. Our two boats, lashed together entered the dark channel, overhung by trees. The water was full of black and dangerous snags. I called to the oarsmen to give way with all their might. Seizing the steering oar myself which felt in my hands as light as a feather, going in sudden twists and turns to port and lee, going through the crooked channel with scarce room to pass between the snags, we eventually came out safe.[2]

An old boatman who witnessed this passage thought them mighty favored by someone to have gotten two boats through Devil's Race Course (Dead Man's Shoals) without mishap.

This incident was not, however, the most heart-stopping experience for Eliza Julia. Below Cincinnati, one of the small boys, Richard, fell overboard. A Mr. Hayward, a young man from Oxfordshire traveling with the Flowers, jumped in after him and both man and child disappeared. Hayward grabbed Richard's collar and swimming under the boat brought him to the surface on the other side unharmed except for the drenching. There were other less frightening, but none the less frustrating, incidents. The crew of four oarsmen deserted in Cincinnati, making it necessary to recruit others. Vivid memories of the anxiety of having to attend to a newborn child and two active little boys, the desertion of the crew, and the dangerous passages that George had to steer them through led Eliza Julia to recommend to John Andrews that Charles should travel by steamboat because of the availability of steamboats with dependable crews. Steamboat travel had come to the river in the previous decade, and as early as 1820 one could travel from Louisville to New Orleans in twenty days.

William Owen, son of Robert Owen, gives a graphic description in his diary of his travels with his father on the Ohio River, the details of which may be considered typical for the time:

Friday 10 Dec. 1824

On awakening we found ourselves at Louisville. Nearly 680 miles from Pittsburgh, having completed the voyage in three days and 16 hours including all stoppages—A little before dark we landed on the Indiana side to take in wood having sailed about 25 miles down the river.—Wood here sells for $1.37½ per cord. We took in 9 cords which feed 6 boilers required for one piston. The power of the engine of 70 or 80 horse power. They consume about a cord in an hour. In the *Favourite* the paddles are quite behind the boat and the machinery aft of the cabins. This is convenient except as regards a sharp turn, in which case the side paddles are more effective. The cabin is small, containing only 16 berths. We had 6 ladies besides 3 children including 2 who came on board when we stopped to take on wood.—The deck is covered in and contains several bedsteads. Great part was filled with cargo, but besides other deck passengers, they contrived to stowaway 47 slaves, going down to be sold. About 10 o'clock mattresses began to be laid down for those who had no berths.[3]

Journey by water was both easier and cheaper than travel overland. Water remained the popular route of travel to the west for many years.

There were, however, alternative routes to those taken by the Flowers. The opening of the Erie Canal in 1825 made travel on the Great Lakes an option. Travelers en route to southeastern Illinois could take the Hudson River from New York to the canal and from there to Erie, Pennsylvania. From Erie, one went overland to Pittsburgh to embark there on the Ohio River. The other route began at New Orleans, whence travelers could take a steamboat up the Mississippi and Ohio rivers to Illinois. As late as 1844 an Englishman identified only as "S," who came to Albion, wrote to his family in England,

If you would give me my former situation, and pay my passage back, we are all in one mind, we would not return. We met with our inconveniences, but what of that? As to our travels, I think I have related them up to New York: from there to Albany we proceeded in a tow boat, one hundred and sixty miles, paid 1 dollar each, luggage free; from Albany to Buffalo, three hundred and sixty-three miles, 3 dollars each, luggage free, five days on our passage; from Buffalo to Erie, on the Lake Erie, ninety miles, 1 dollar 50 cents each, luggage free. If you come this way, and the winds be high, you will find it as unpleasant as the sea; a steamboat leaves every morning, they told us. There was a canal cutting from Cleveland to Cincinnati, some said it was finished, but others said not; I should think if it be completed when you come it would be the best way, as we found water conveyance to be a great deal cheaper, and much pleasanter, than land. At Erie we engaged a waggon and six horses, bearing seventeen bells, for 3½ cents per lb.; 2 dollars 50 cents for each woman, one hundred and sixty miles to Pittsburgh; but the man, for his own interest, took us a way that brought us to Beavers, thirty miles below Pittsburgh, and here we had to stop three days waiting for a boat, and being weary we bought an old ferry boat, and got some pine and fitted it up so we could lodge in it, and we ran down near a thousand miles in fifteen days, and lay by nights, and stopped at Mt. Vernon, and then sent G. Curtis to Mr. Lambert's for we could not engage a team, and Mr. Lambert was so kind as to come eighty-six miles, and brought us up here, and only charged expenses, and we arrived on the 10th of July.—We think you had better come by New Orleans. Your baggage will be to shift from the ship to the steamboat, and then you run at once to Shawnee-town or Mount Vernon. If it be wet, don't come to Mt. Vernon, as there are some muddy rivers to cross. If you come this way, by New Orleans, I mean, you will perhaps have to be nine weeks on the sea; but then you will have more room in the ship, and less trouble in shifting your things; and when you do shift them, mind and look if you have your number, for there were some people on the canal, through carelessness, lost two boxes. It would be well to paint your name upon them, and number them. I dare say that by Orleans, if you mind at Liverpool, will be the cheapest way to come and in the shortest time.[4]

George Flower, in giving advice to emigrants, pointed out that most Englishmen still did not realize the vastness of the United States and fell into the error of comparing it to England and therefore arrived at the wrong location in America. He advised that southern Illinois should be selected for future residence since the route by New Orleans was the most convenient. But, he cautioned, there were fewer ships to New Orleans than to New York. One could choose to go from New York to Philadelphia overland, which was but six hours travel; and that from Philadelphia there were three routes to the Ohio River which George believed to be the "grand thoroughfare to all the Western States."[5]

By 1833, there were many more people in Illinois and in other parts of the West, and the demand for internal improvements was loud in the land. Farmers needed to get their harvest to markets. They needed other avenues of transportation in addition to rivers. Such necessity created great interest in canals and in road building, but the completion of a good system was far in the future.

Travel was difficult by any standard, but that did not deter people like the Flowers. Eliza Julia told John of her trip with George on the National Road. This road, from Terre Haute to St. Louis, followed what is now U.S. 40 across the state of Illinois. Before 1820, the National Road had been finished westward sixty-two miles from Cumberland, Maryland, to Uniontown, Pennsylvania. It was gradually extended farther and farther west, and at the time Eliza Julia mentioned it (1833), the National Road was a "track laid down and being worked" in Illinois. The amount of traffic made this route more discernible than many, and inns and taverns were more frequent, but the road was far from perfect. Writing in his later years, George described a trip with Eliza Julia on the National Road (possibly the same trip she mentioned, or one very like it) and said,

Following its course westward, we were suddenly arrested by a broad sheet of water, which we dared not enter and could not go around. The moon set. We were in darkness. Wet through, exposed to a keen north wind, without the slightest shelter, we stood by the side of our horses and waited the termination of this dreary night.[6]

It was some time before good roads were generally available. As late as 1842, Charles Dickens wrote of a portion of the road to St. Louis, "It had no variety but in depth. Now it was only half over the wheels, now it hid the axletree, and now the coach sank down in it almost to the windows."[7]

Since travel was most easily undertaken on the rivers, the movement of people and goods necessarily followed the river banks. Population maps of the early settlement of Illinois show that the first communities grew along the Ohio, the Mississippi, and their tributaries. In these towns, merchants and agents for the farmers set up their businesses. One such person was Mr. Docker in Shawneetown. Eliza Julia told John about Mr. Docker, the Flowers' agent, who with others like him helped with marketing produce, procuring goods that were not available locally, forwarding mail, and honoring bank drafts. In addition to Mr. Docker in Shawneetown, Thomas Bakewell of Cincinnati and Jeremiah Warder, the Flowers' Quaker friend in Philadelphia, also served the family as agents. Warder, working with agents like Docker along the river, made it possible for business to be conducted between the populous East and the sparsely settled West. Through these arrangements, shipments of supplies were sent to the settlers, guests were directed to the English Prairie, and produce from the settlement was sent to distant markets.

By July Charles Andrews had not yet arrived in Albion. His aunt was concerned about the delay. Eliza Julia had a right to feel "some anxiety lest something should have befallen him," as she put it in her next letter. She knew from her own experience that travel down the Ohio River was often very dangerous, and not only because of the shoals and currents. Although many of the more notorious outlaws like the Harpe brothers were dead before the 1830s, there were still many rough characters who made their living by ambushing travelers. Under the pretense of offering help, either piloting their flatboats or guiding their wagons, they ambushed the travelers in secluded spots, robbing and often killing them, making the stretch of the Ohio River from the mouth of the Wabash to its confluence with the Mississippi particularly rough.[8] This may have been the reason why Eliza Julia always alerted Mr. Docker, the Shawneetown agent, to the arrival of their expected guests. She explained this concern in her letter of June (or July) 16, 1833.

June [sic] 16, 1833

Near Albion Edwards County

My dear John,

I duly recieved yours dated May 13th informing me that Charles would leave New York in 3 or 4 weeks for Albion. This news gave us pleasure and Mr. Flower and myself both wrote to Mr. Docker of ShawneeTown informing him that he would see Charles in 6 or 7 weeks from the date of yours and requesting him to pay him every attention and to find a speedy and comfortable conveyance to our house with all speed—it is now the 16th of July[9] and we have heard nothing of him and I cannot help feeling some anxiety lest something should have befallen him,—if any thing should have detain'd him with you you would surely have written me word and if he set off from New York at the time you proposed he will surely be here in a few days, at any rate let me hear from you upon the reciept of this—and I will write to you directly Charles arrives I have prepared his Chamber his Bed his Closet, and arranged everything for his Comfort and the Children ask every day—"Mama when will Cousin Charles come?"—Charles first employment after his arrival will be to assist his Uncle in the Mill, this is a very Clean nice healthy business—and if Charles proves expert in learning the Trade and should happen to like it it will probably fall into his hands on a future day—Mr. Flower will give him all the instruction he requires and I will make him a happy home—You need feel no anxiety for his Welfare as from the moment he arrives we take him as one of our own Children, I should however wish that he should keep up a close correspondance with you that you may know exactly his situation here and inform his poor Mother—I have now something to say to you about your own concerns—You mention that your health is not very good in New York I am very sorry for it and I wish to tell you that there is now for Sale—a very neat compact Tavern and land at Maysville in this State—it lies 30 miles North West of us— and on the High Road from Vincennes St.Louis Vandalia and Albion—it is extremely well situated for Business and the House is in good repute the Country round is fine and healthy prairie— there are also some Public Offices mark'd to the Concern which the Present owner would give up with the premises viz—County Clarck, Judge of Probate and the Post office bringing in from 150 to 200 dollars per annum independant of the Tavern which taking the year thro—(for at some seasons there is much more travelling than at others)—from 3 to 4 hundred dollars per year—but supposing we say 3 Hundred and the Public Offices 150 that would be an income of $450 per year which in the Country is a pretty income—with great room for improving and enlarging if you please—for these premises consisting of a neat new frame House of 5 Rooms—a Kitchen Paddock Good Stabling for 8 or 10 Horses and other out buildings all under fence and in good repair—The owner asks one Thousand dollars to be paid in quarterly installments in 2 or 3 years. The first installment to be paid next May. It occured to me that it might be a very good thing for you both for your health and your pocket if you and your Wife happen'd to think so—If you should turn it over in your mind you can let me know and I will then write you every particular—I have in the meantime requested Mr Ridgeway the owner who is also a friend of ours to give me the first refusal for you—I should like you extremely to be near us—if it was also for your benifit my time is gone give my kind love to your Wife and boy I'll endeavour for the future to remember your dignity and not call you boys but if you are old men what then am I?

Your affectionate Aunt

Eliza J. Flower

all send love

In this letter, one can again see evidence of Eliza Julia's very good sense of business as she described the opportunities for John at Maysville.

The town of Vandalia, mentioned by Eliza Julia in this letter as lying on the National Road, had become the seat of government in Illinois in 1818, so anyone from the English Settlement having state business traveled this road. Maysville is now the town of Clay City in Illinois on Illinois highway 50. In the 1820s there was more than a casual relationship between Maysville and Albion since several Albion merchants, including Hugh Ronalds, Eliza Julia's brother-in-law, had stores in Maysville as well as in Albion. Perhaps because it lay on the High Road between Vincennes and St. Louis, and Albion did not, Maysville received more traffic.

Neither Maysville nor Vandalia, however, was as important to the settlement as Shawneetown. Because it played such an important role in the development of the English Settlement and for so many other people who moved into Illinois, it deserves description here. In 1814 the United States Government had designated Kaskaskia and Shawneetown as land offices. It was to the latter that Birkbeck went to purchase his and Flower's properties on the Boltenhouse Prairie. When Illinois became a state in 1817 its population was only 35,000, and only two settlements, Shawneetown and Kaskaskia, could claim any resemblance to established communities.[9] John Woods, one of the early members of the English Settlement, described Shawneetown as it was when he arrived in 1819.

In the morning we moved opposite to Shawneetown, and anchored close to some rocks, amongst keel-boats, arks, &c., some of them for sale. Many disembark here to go by land to Kaskaskia, and St. Louis, on the Mississippi river; and some for the English Settlement at the Prairies. It is subject to floods, and that retards its growth. It is the nearest inhabited spot below the mouth of the Wabash, and in the neighbourhood of the United States Saline works, where about 300,000 bushels of salt are made annually. It is the county town of Gallatin, and has a land office for the sale of the government lands, situated in the south east part of the state of the Illinois; extending 80 or 90 miles from the Ohio river towards the north; these united causes draw many to it and make it a brisk place. There is a bank called the "Bank of Illinois", in good repute, many stores, and several taverns; the principal one, the Steam-boat Hotel, kept by Mr. Hobson from the north of England. There are about 80 houses, mostly of wood, and a wooden jail. The situation of the town is handsome; but being surrounded by low land, that is likely to be inundated, it is rather unhealthy, at least it was so when we were there.[10]

Captain Christopher Hobson, mentioned by Mr. Woods, had kept one of the first stores on the English Prairie. Encouraged and vouched for by Morris Birkbeck, he set up a shop near Wanborough as early as 1818, getting merchandise from Harmonie. He soon faced financial difficulties with his store and moved to Shawneetown, which, although it had no courthouse, church, or school, was the busiest frontier settlement nearby. There he became the agent for the Harmonist Society in August 1821. Although problems of credit and credibility continued to haunt him, he was the storekeeper for the Harmonists until he became ill. He then returned to Albion to seek medical treatment; he died there on 7 May 1823.

Theodore Pease wrote of Shawneetown, "The most important function which the town performed was that of furnishing a buying and shipping point for country produce and a distributing point for store goods."[11] He added,

In the Illinois of 1818, Shawneetown seemed to hold a favorable position as the gateway, a fact which had been recognized by the United States government by the designation of the town as a port of entry. It was the natural Illinois entrepot for the eastern part of the state and for the country up the tributaries of the Wabash.[12]

By 1833, Shawneetown was still an important center for life in southeastern Illinois and therefore a most logical destination for Eliza Julia to set for Charles. The Shawneetown Charles would have seen would have been different from the rough river port of the early days as described by James Hall, editor and journalist of the time. He wrote,

Before the introduction of steamboats upon this river, its immense commerce was chiefly carried on by means of barges—large boats, calculated to descend as well as ascend the stream, and which required many hands to navigate them. Each barge carried from thirty to forty boatmen, and a number of these boats frequently sailed in company. The arrival of such a squadron at a small town was the certain forerunner of a riot. Shawneetown is now a quiet place, exhibiting much of the activity of business, but with little dissipation and still less of outbreaking disorder.[13]

The Ohio River, although no longer the only route to the West, was a direct route from Pittsburgh to Shawneetown, and from there it was but a relatively short distance to Albion.

Chapter 4

"I have educated them as far as I am capable."

Eliza Julia

T HE BEST OF PLANS are often modified, and those of Charles Andrews's coming to Albion were no exception. In her next letter, in spite of her earlier reluctance to take Charles into her home, Eliza Julia revealed her fear that something had happened to him and he might not ever come to join them. Perhaps her disappointment was deepened because her correspondence with John Rutt Andrews had produced an upwelling of a real sense of family, a feeling of which she had been deprived since coming to America. A door partially opened seemed to close, naturally a disappointment. She must have known that her unorthodox marriage to George probably made it impossible for her ever to visit her family in England.

Eliza Julia had grown up in a strict family environment. Although hers was a politically liberal family, and one that valued education highly, it was also a most respectable family that undoubtedly took a dim view of her bigamous alliance. Her grandfather, Mordecai, was a Congregational minister educated at Kings Head Academy and ordained in 1743. Her father, also named Mordecai, was educated for the ministry at Mile End Academy. One of her aunts was married to a minister, known for his piety; and an older brother, Edward, who had been educated for the ministry since he was a lad at Hoxton Academy, had an L.L.B. from the University of Glasgow. In 1817, when Eliza Julia married George, her brother

Edward, having already spent eight years at the University of Glasgow as a Dr. Williams Scholar, was within two years of his degree. Since their father had died when Eliza Julia was about seven years old, it was probably an older brother's family that shunned her, and he might well have encouraged her other brothers to distance themselves from her.

Eliza Julia's strength of character and her love for George that led her to enter into such an unusual marriage must have separated her from her family in spirit as well as in miles of ocean and land. The warmth of her letters to John Rutt Andrews suggests the possibility that from time to time she might have wished to see or hear from them. In the next letter, her comment that her daughter Rosa reminds her of John's sister, Jemima, further supports this idea. Although her hopes for a reunion with some of the family seemed thwarted, characteristically she pressed on with life and the work at hand, keeping the door open for future developments.

Having been a member of a well-educated family, Eliza Julia was very much aware of the absence of educational opportunities on the English Prairie. From her letters we obtain a glimpse of education on the frontier of 1833. The English view of education was understandably different from that of the Americans who came to settle southeastern Illinois, because of the differences in their backgrounds. Roy A. Billington wrote,

The predominantly southern character of Illinois' early migration cannot be overemphasized. In 1818, when the first survey was taken, 38% of the settlers were from the South Atlantic seaboard, almost 37% from Kentucky and Tennessee, 13% from the Middle States, 3% from New England and 9% from abroad.[1]

Englishmen who, like the Flowers, had been well educated at home, were concerned that the second generation be as literate as their parents. They were engaged in a struggle against the anti-intellectualism of the majority of the frontiersmen. Eliza Julia put it well when she wrote that Emma must not "grow up in these wild woods in perfect ignorance of what the world is made of and what is going on in it," and she described steps to be taken to provide for the education of her children.

Christina Tillson, a New Englander who moved into central Illinois about this same time, reported the attitude against which she and women like Eliza Julia had to contend by quoting a frontiersman:

Twant so bad for men to read, for there was a heap of time when they couldnt work out, and could jest sit by the fire; and if a man had books and kerred to read he mought; but women had no business to hurtle away their time, case they could allus find something to du, and there had been a heap of trouble in old Kaintuck with some rich men's gals that had learned to write. They was sent to school, and were high larnt, and cud write letters almost as well as a man, and would write to young fellows, and bless your soul, get a match fixed up before their father and mother knowed a hait about it.[2]

That Eliza Julia saw education for her children, boys and girls, as precious is easily understood in the light of her own education. She had a nanny and a governess as a child, had studied French and art, and had learned to play the pianoforte. She was a good pianist and an avid reader. When she was growing up, she had been encouraged to think for herself. Her children remembered that she tried to teach her daughters exactly as she had been taught and what she had been taught (with the exception of French). She was an accomplished needlewoman and made many pieces of fancy work for both Prairie House and Park House. She regaled her children with tales of England, and in her last years, when her eyesight was failing, they reciprocated by reading to her, for her love of books never diminished.[3]

Park House Near Albion

September 1st 1833

My dear John,

I was nearly 100 miles from home when your letter arrived and did not recieve it until it was too late to answer by return of post. I was both sorry and glad at its contents. I think Charles was quite right to take and keep so eligible a situation but we all feel much disappointed to learn that he wasnt coming to join us—however tell him with our united loves to him that at any time or hour when circumstances may make it desirable for him to change his situation he will find a welcome here with us. I am extremely glad to hear of your success in business and so long as your health will permit you to live in a city I would on no account advise you to let go so good a certainty for an uncertainty, for every new business or profession must be an uncertainty for a time—The Tavern I wrote you about at Maysville was sold last week to a young English couple just imported from London—how they will succeed I know not for both of them are full of Island of England prejudices and neither of them possesses any common sense. I have been extremely engaged since I wrote you last in looking out for a good boarding school for our two eldest daughters Emma and Rosamond and preparing them for their removal next week their father and myself take them to Vandalia, the seat of government in this State 80 miles from Albion. Its a long distance to send such Children from home but I have educated them as far as I am capable and Emma who is a very promising girl of fourteen—and as tall as myself, must not grow up and live in these wild woods in perfect ignorance of what the world is made of and what is going on in it—Rosa is just such a looking little girl as I remember your sister Jemima 9 years old. I send her partly to be a companion to Emma and still hoping that she will make good use of her time, her capacity is good and she is extremely anxious to improve herself. I feel a great deal about their going away so far from home, but I know of no alternative— our two eldest boys ought now to be at a good school but we cannot find one in this State that we like and I think it more than probable that we shall send them next year to New York, if we do I should like to place them with or near you but of that hereafter—What do you think about sending for your brother George? I should like to have him with us—the very name George is dear to me. My brother, his uncle I dearly loved—and my husband's name is George—I have no George of my own because Mr. Flower's eldest son is George—if George comes over to you and you think well of it, I will endeavour to send you the money to bear his expenses to us here and then make him my own— describe him in your next. You must not be hurt or surprised when you do not hear from me—for I have so much to attend to that I believe I work harder and have less time than any other person in the settlement and now my time is less my own than ever for since I wrote you last, we have changed our abode. Mr. Flower's mother is very aged and often sick and as she depends entirely upon me to nurse her we have thought it better to live with her for I could not attend to my own house and hers too—I therefore brought my own servants here and take the entire managment of the house and board her in it at a certain sum per annum—this has long been her wish and choice and she is very happy and much better in health already and I am well satisfied tho' no place in the world will ever be so dear to me as our own original cabins where I have been so very very happy for so many years! This Estate and house etc fall to my husband at the death of his mother and now I have two families to attend to instead of one and I have to recieve her friends and acquaintances as well as my own, therefore you may imagine that if my time was occupied in my own house it is doubly so in this.—Write to me often and let me know your doings from time to time. Request Charles to write to me and give me a little account of himself—I yearn to see you both and your kind good Wife and Boy. You are a happy fellow to have so affectionate a wife—mind that you always love and cherish her as the very apple of your eye—you will never find any friend to take her place give her my kind love—I have a wonderful curiosity to see New York and all the Eastern cities. I shall consider it a crime not to see them before I die! but I cannot go so far from home unless I could induce old Mrs Flower to accompany us which I fear she is too infirm ever to do but if ever things should so turn up I shall pounce upon you and Charles directly and claim kindred. Haven't you a curiosity to see me? When I left England I was a blooming girl, now I am an old woman, the mother of twelve children, grey headed and almost toothless. I am of a happy temperament and have always been and am now very healthy—my delight and joy is in my home. I believe my husband doats on me, if he doesn't I doat on him—His mother always treats me with great consideration—I on my part show her all attention her age and widowhood require. My dress is always black with a white turban! I forgot to tell you that my age is 42 or 43—and I desire after this minute description of myself that if you should meet me in the streets of New York, that you will immediately salute me without any further introduction. Of course you know that in countenance I am like the rest of family not wanting in the noseway! then my dear nephew—I dare not say boy! God bless you and yours—your Uncle sends kind wishes to you all as do your cousins with your affectionate Aunt

Eliza J. Flower

Give my fond love to your father mother and family when you write again. I remember Jemima as well as though I saw her yesterday.[4]

Few schools existed on the prairies of early Illinois because of the sparseness of the homesteads, and the quality of instruction was limited by the absence of well-prepared teachers. Solon J. Buck, discussing this subject, quoted John Mason Peck, Baptist missionary and one of the best-informed men on the frontier:

At least one-third of the schools were really a public nuisance, and did the people more harm than good; one-third about balanced the account by doing as much good as harm, and perhaps one-third were advantageous to the community in various degrees.[5]

Although some good teachers were hired from the East Coast, they were not well received by the pioneers, whose pride was hurt by this importation even though it was generally agreed that most of the indigenous teachers were poorly educated. Theodore Pease wrote,

The earliest schools were most casual affairs. They were kept by drunkards, by men with the barest smattering of knowledge, unfitted for other purposes by physical or moral defects.[6]

In Albion a subscription school was opened in 1819 by Oswald Warrington, whose specialty was penmanship, and it was said many men of the next generation owed good, legible handwriting to him. William Owen recorded a visit to the school in his diary.

We proceeded then to Mr. Warrenton's [sic] school, in a small room in a stone building, where we found him instructing about 15 boys and girls. He showed us some good specimens of writing and told us he made the children take places.[7]

The school did not last long. Warrington was licensed for $6 in 1823 to keep a tavern and vend spirits. He did, in fact, become alcoholic to such an extent that in 1825 when he applied to be included in Robert Owen's New Society, he was to be admitted conditionally only "after 4 months of sober life."[8]

John Love "kept school in a little house on West Main Street."[9] The next school in the settlement was a log school house, built in 1820 some three miles from Albion at Little

Prairie, and another was constructed a few miles north of Albion deep in the country. None of these would have been of any use to George and Eliza Julia for their children since none were in the immediate vicinity of Park House and Prairie House and because the Flower children could be educated by their parents well beyond the scope of the early schoolmasters in such schools.

The state of Illinois took its first action on education in 1818 in a bill introduced by Nathaniel Pope, which among other things stipulated that 3 percent of government land sales should be used for education, that monies from Section 16 in each township should be used for schools, and that funds from a whole township should be used for an educational seminary. On 15 January 1825, the General Assembly passed an "Act Providing for the Establishment of Free Schools" that would have been of great benefit to all had the General Assembly chosen to fund and put into actuality such a forward-looking piece of legislation. The law of 1825 was not really effective. George Flower wrote that

no matter what laws may exist on the subject, or what school fund may lie in the treasury of the State, if there were not children sufficient within a mile of a schoolhouse, there can be no school. Also, in a town or village, however humble, a school is soon got up, and is often a spontaneous growth.[10]

In 1837 George and Eliza Julia, with other literary-minded people, decided that education of high quality must be provided. Thus on 29 January 1838 a public meeting was held to establish a public school and to provide a suitable building to house a school and a fine library. This building was to be erected on the southeast section of the public square; a constitution was adopted, and Eliza Julia and George (as well as George's mother, Elizabeth) were among the eleven persons signing the document. The school was to be supported by donations, annual subscriptions, and the sale of scholarships or shares at twenty-five dollars each.[11] Mrs. Richard Flower and George Flower each bought ten shares. Each share would allow one child to attend the school as long as necessary. Non-shareholders could send their children to the school for $5 a quarter. Orphans and destitute children, utterly without

means of subscribing, were to receive full benefit of the
school on application, provided that the means of the school
justified their admission and that their admission did not de-
prive the regular pupils of instruction. The building was to be
used as a school five days a week and on Saturday and Sunday as a reading room from 10 A.M. to 9 P.M. It was not until
September 1838, five years after Eliza Julia's letter to John,
that this, the first permanent schoolhouse, was opened in Albion. It was a two-story brick building, a testimony of the
Flowers' dedication to education.[12]

Until the fruition in 1838 of these hopes and plans for a
real school, the Flower children were educated by their parents and relatives. Eliza Julia was proud of her work as a
teacher. In her letter of 2 August 1834 she wrote, "We have an
excellent collection of Books and take several Home and foreign News papers—they give you a summary kind of
knowledge."

When the children outgrew these lessons they were sent
away, if possible to academies and seminaries in other areas.
In 1827, George Flower had sent his son George to the
McClure School in New Harmony to learn a trade. He did not
stay long, because his father was not pleased with the
school.[13] Shortly after Eliza Julia's letter of September 1833,
Alfred and Camillus Flower were taught by George's sister
Kate and her husband, Hugh Ronalds, who the family
thought were particularly capable and who had done an ex-
ceptionally fine job with their own children. The boys probably never went to New York to John's supervision, a
possibility that Eliza Julia suggested in her letter to him.
George Flower's strong opinions about schools were in con-
flict with current practice. He firmly believed that children
should be allowed physical exercise. He disapproved of making children perform, that is, recite. He did not approve of
rote learning.

Respect for learning was an important characteristic of
the Flower family. Since good schools were not available in
the area at the time, the family resourcefully turned to books,
magazines, and some texts that were prepared especially for
young people and that were already in their library or could
be obtained by mail. Early in the establishment of the settle-

ment, Richard Flower had given some of his own books and gathered others from friends in England to create the first public library in Albion, and for that matter in Illinois. Eliza Julia's sons Camillus and Alfred thus had access to their grandfather Richard Flower's extensive personal library. Richard Flower had "brought with him a very large and costly library, largely historical, biographical and theological. . . . His library was as wide in its scope as that of his own free spirit of inquiry."[14]

Always strong for education, Richard Flower was pleased when he made a convert to reading. In a letter of 1820, he wrote,

You would have been much amused if you had been with us a few weeks since, when I had a visit from Capt. Burke, a sensible and intelligent backwoodsman—"there wife," said he, "did you ever see such fixings?" He felt the paper, looked into a mirror over our chimney piece and gazed with amazement. But turning from these sights to the library,—"Now," said he to my wife, "does the old gentleman", (for that is my title here), "read all those books?" "Yes," said she, "he has read most of them." "Why, if I was to read half of them, I should drive all the little sense in my head out of it." I replied that we read to increase our sense and our knowledge; but this untutored son of nature could not conceive of this 'til I took down a volume of Shaw's *Zoology*. "You, Mr. Burke, are an old hunter, and have met with many snakes in your time. I never saw above one in my life; now if I can tell you about your snakes and deer, and bears and wolves, as much or more than you know, you will see the use of books." I read to him a description of a rattle-snake, and then shewed him a coloured plate, and so on. His attention was arrested, and his thirst for knowledge fast increasing.[14]

Perhaps Pease's description of education in Illinois as "casual" is not completely accurate for 1842, but from William Dobell's letter of that year it is clear that schooling was not yet well established everywhere:

My late School near the Village Prairie is broken up—the School House sold and removed to a distance in Village Prairie to serve for a Township School. I have been staying at Sister Craig's above a month, but in the meantime have been able to organize a School at Graysville a Town on the Wabash 10 miles from Albion where I shall commence on Monday next with Eleven Scholars already subscribed for, and a good prospect of an increase; I hope this change will better my circumstances, as my late School did not yield sufficient for the expenses of my board, Clothing etc. during the past year. I leave it when everything is settled, worse off than I was 12 months ago; it was only during the first 12 or 18 months that I was able to save anything & that not much. Keeping School here is an uncertain employment as to its continuance. In some situations the people are satisfied with a School of 3 or 6 months continuance during the winter and it is no uncommon thing in Summer to see School Teachers anxiously seeking for employment of some kind. It is unusual for a Teacher to continue for 2 or 3 years in the same place as I have done and Mr. Harwick who opened a School in Albion before I came is here still and likely to continue. I hope my introduction to Graysville may lead to a settlement there as the Town & neighborhood will be able to supply a succession of Scholars.—Mrs. Craig's School is in a flourishing state—she now has 25 scholars. Lucy & Henry are well, & getting forward in their Education, but not so fast as I could wish to see them. Your liberal and enlightened friends will feel pleased to hear, that the people in this part of the country appear to feel an increasing interest on the subject of Education. New Schools are erecting, & Schools have already increased in various Districts around Albion, & there does not appear to be any lack of competent Teachers to conduct them—and I hope the time is not far distant when there will hardly be found a young man or woman who has not at least learnt to read & write. This is a pleasing Subject of observation & of anticipation, for Political & Civil Liberty without knowledge and education may in many cases lead to Licentiousness and disregard of Order & good Government.[16]

Granting that the life of a schoolteacher was hard, by 1842 Dobell was also reflecting the increasing interest in and support of better schools by the public in the vicinity of Albion. It was during the 1840s and 1850s that "public support for free education and for the proper preparation of teachers was won."[17] But that was ten years in the future.

Eliza Julia's next letter gives considerable insight into how parents, with the use of appropriate reading materials, could educate their own children when good schools were not at hand.

Mount Carmel

March 23, (mailed Ap. 14) 1834

My dear John,

I duly recieved your last letter and should have answered it long ago but for a severe and protracted illness from which myself and 2 of our Children are just recovering and recover'd—I am now on a little journey with my Husband for the still benifit of my health and the pleasure of his Company and being detain'd by the Weather at a Tavern on the road—I am glad to make the time pass agreeably by chatting with you—I give you and your Wife joy upon the birth of your daughter who by the way must be a great fat girl by this time—I hope her being called after me will not harm her—but I fear it will never do her any good! for dear John "what's in a name"—"a rose by any other name will smell as sweet however I thank you and your Wife for the Compliment wh I am sure was kindly meant—and is kindly recieved—With regard to our two Eldest boys—we have had so much sickness—this Winter amongst the Children that I do not think that I shall ever make up my mind to send them so far from home, we have felt that Rosamond and Emma are too far off—and as the School does not in many respects answer our expectations—we intend to bring them home this summer. Both Mr. Flower and myself had taken a great deal of pains with Emma before we sent her to School—and we find that she already knows as much as her present Governess—The one we placed her under having taken to herself a Husband and placed a younger sister in her stead which does not suit our views for the benifit of our Children—Mr. Flower went the other day to Vandalia to see them—and found them happy enough—and well taken care of—but not improving in their studies as we could wish—he therefore made arrangements as I said before for their return and [as] it regards the boys I think at present they will remain at the day school where they have been for the last 5 months and where Alfred the Eldest had made considerable progress—he is nearly 12 years of age—and for a *Backwoods Boy* is tolerably informed—he writes a pretty good hand, is learning to compose, has a wonderful turn for reading of *Battles* by Sea and by land and I expect some day will march off for a Sailor or a Soldier—That is if he was sure of being always *Victorious* for he cannot bear to be defeated in any thing—and therefore I tell him he must work very hard both in body and mind or half the world will get before him and he will die in despair at last! We take in Parley's Magazine for the Children which is a very cheap and very useful publication both for young and old and I think it very benificial to Charles being both instructive and amusing—and cheap—$1 per annum in 12 numbers—if you have never heard of it do get one number and examine it—I presume it is to be bought at any of the Booksellers where Books for *Youth* are chiefly sold. I cannot now remember who are the Publishers but Parley has written several very useful books for youth particularly, an excellent Geography and I think a Grammer[18]—I am sorry Charles cannot make up his mind to write to me, the very first leisure I have I shall write to him to encourage him to make the best of the opportunities he has had—and endeavour to improve himself in every way that he can in order to advance himself in future life for as you very justly observe want of Early Education may be a great drawback to promotion but then if we have done our best to improve ourselves it may be our *Misfortune* but cannot be considered as our fault—If anything turns up in the Rugg Trade which you seem to think possible and Charles should be out of employ and still he should like to come to us We will give him all the chances with our own Children and push him along in the World as much as is in our power—and make him as happy as we can and he in return must do for us what he can—tell him this with our love to him—I am rejoiced to hear that you are going on so nicely—and cannot see why you shouldn't enter into partnership with your present employer if he wishes it and you think it would increase your *Gains* and not injure your health. Give my love to your Mother and Father when you write I am very glad your Mothers health improves—no doubt but the prospect of her Children settled well is a great relief to her mind tell me in your next if you have heard of your Brother George and whether there is a prospect of his coming into this Country—Write to me whenever you can—I am always pleased to hear from you—you must not be surprised if my letters are "long and far between" for I believe that I have less leisure than any other woman in this State or any other state for besides having my own family to provide for I have the entire responsibility and care of Mr. F. Mother upon me as also 2 children of my Husbands Sister who is gone to England for her health[19] This makes my family 12 in number besides hired House Servants and farm servants—and more *Company* than I could sometime name—my youngest Boy can just run alone the next to him but 11 months older and I expect to be confined again in June—You may therefore judge that I cannot have much time either of body or mind—indeed I sometimes think that we must leave the large House wh we now inhabit and retire to a cabin in the wood wh would be much more to my taste because it would give me more time to attend to my Husband and Children and we sh'd also be living at much less expense than we do now My kind love to your wife and little ones, and long may you prosper and live happily together—I should like extremely to go to New York but with more babys at hand I fear it is almost out of the question for me at present—if my Husband should go there this summer as he still sometimes talks of doing—he will of course find you out

I am dear John

Your aff'tte Aunt

Eliza J. Flower

Sunday April 7th

I have only time to acknowledge and thank you for your news paper and wish you all success in your partnership—I will write again soon my love to you all.

It is impressive that amidst all these activities she still found time to write to her nephew John. Clearly she was pleased that John had named his new daughter for her, which must have been another small link to her own family in England.

George's strong convictions about the educational process may partially explain why he took Rosamond and Emma out of the school they had been attending in Vandalia as described in Eliza Julia's letter. Besides, owing to what she had learned from her parents at home, Emma knew more than her teacher in Vandalia. Although two of Eliza Julia's girls were sent away to school, and the experiment proved to be unsuccessful, the boys attended a local day school, probably because their labor was needed to keep the Flower enterprises operating. That the girls should have had such an opportunity reveals a great deal about the attitudes of George and Eliza Julia, because the girls, too, could have been helpful in a hundred ways at home, and the conventional wisdom of pioneer Illinois was that girls did not need much education. Emma and Rosamond, although not getting the quality of education for which their parents had hoped, remained in Vandalia until the end of the spring term.

Eliza Julia's daily tasks and the burden of caring for George's mother and managing the affairs of Park House did not dim her determination to rear her children as educated persons. Such an attitude was not common among those settled on the prairie, and many of those who wished for education for their children were unable to make it happen.

Chapter 5

*"American females have a sleight of hand in getting through
house-work of all kinds without apparent labour."*

George Flower

I<small>N HER LETTER OF 23 MARCH</small> 1834, Eliza Julia revealed the
pressures of managing Park House through her expressed
wish to be back in her original home in Albion or one like it.
Park House, constructed with Marden, Richard Flower's
house in England in mind, was an extraordinary place, an
English country house on the wild Illinois prairie. It was
George who supervised its building in the English Settlement in 1818 while Richard and his wife, Elizabeth, waited
with friends in Lexington, Kentucky. Park House was the
grandest place for miles around, and since hospitality was a
hallmark of the Flower family they and their house became
well known. Park House almost always had visitors, some for
an evening or a day and others for a week or a month at a
time. When Fanny Wright and her sister, Camilla, came to Albion from New Harmony in 1825, they lived with George and
Eliza Julia in Prairie House. When George and Fanny Wright
went to found Nashoba early in the fall, Camilla stayed on in
Eliza Julia's home until February 1826. In addition to business
associates and friends who became guests at Park House,
many travelers from England and Europe who came to see
the West as well as the eastern part of the new United States
of America visited the Flowers. Even after 1825, when New
Harmony took the center of the stage, visitors still came to see
Park House. It was famous as the most magnificent home of

its time west of the Alleghenies and as the home of one of the founders of the settlement; and it was at Park House on 1 January 1825, that Robert Owen and George Rapp finally agreed to the sale and purchase of Harmonie, the town that became New Harmony. Years later, a grandson summed up Park House hospitality: "For thirty years his [Flower's] spacious Park House was never without visitors from every country in Europe and every state in the nation."[1]

Travelers' accounts together with those of George and Richard Flower give a clear picture of Park House as a residence quite different from the log cabins, however embellished, in which others lived. Morris Birkbeck and George Flower lived in log houses. Both were large and gracious but, nonetheless, still constructed of logs. The first brick house in the town of Albion was not built until 1824, and it was considerably more modest than Park House. In June 1820, Richard Flower wrote of his home in the English Settlement, "I have a comfortable habitation, containing four rooms and a hall on the ground floor, and five chambers above; two wings are added which contain a kitchen, china closet, dairy, and an excellent cellar."[2] This may be too modest a statement. Adlard Welby, author of *A Visit to America*, wrote about his visit to Park House in 1819, "In the midst of these wilds the elegant repast and social converse were again, as if by magic, enjoyed."[3] George Flower, whose responsibility it was to oversee the construction of the house, described it as follows:

The body of the house, 50 by 40 feet, covered by a hipped-roof, consisted of four rooms in the lower and the upper story, divided by a hall-passage from north to south. The south front was protected by a broad, well-floored porch, that extended the length of the house. Every room was plastered or papered, and furnished with a good brick chimney and stone hearth. The north front was stuccoed, to resemble stone; the south weatherboarded and painted white. The house was well furnished. Its good proportion, large windows, and Venetian blinds gave it an appearance of the old country rather than the new. It had two wings, one of hewn stone, and the other of brick, used as a kitchen and offices. A well, a cellar, stables, cow-house, and every other convenience of that sort appended. A handsome garden to the south fenced in by an English hawthorn hedge. Thirty acres

Park House, the home of Richard and Elizabeth Fordham Flower, courtesy of the Patricia Flower Martin Collection

Park House, watercolor by George Flower of the home of Richard and Elizabeth Fordham Flower, courtesy of the Chicago Historical Society

of northern woodland was preserved, the underbrush cleared and sowed with blue grass, it had the appearance of a park. Hence, its name—Park House.[4]

In all, it was a large house of eleven or twelve rooms, many dependencies, and extensive lawns and gardens. It was not an easy house to maintain. Each room, above and below, had its own fireplace. Its many large windows with Venetian blinds had to be a housekeeping nightmare. While there were always some servants at Park House, as Eliza Julia wrote in her letters of 1 September 1833 and 23 March 1834, the responsibility for the upkeep of Park House and the maintenance of the tradition of open-handed Flower hospitality fell upon her. Her labors were magnified when she moved from Prairie House into Park House. Entertaining friends and guests of both Richard and George became a heavy burden on her, a fact George Flower appreciated. He wrote in his advice to emigrants,

The American women have a happy knack of rendering a very disagreeable job (or which is rendered so by the old mode of doing it) often-times a very agreeable employment; and in none is it more strikingly displayed than in their mode of getting through with the labour of the wash. Disarray among the females and dismay among the men, combine against all comfort on the awful day, of an English six weeks wash. Here the whole thing is differently performed. The accumulation is not suffered to be so large. Here it is taken little by little, and the mode of attack is very different. The American lady before she begins her morning's wash, first dresses and adorns herself with more than usual care and grace, yielding to the head and hair a little more than ordinary elegance. If a sudden call is made for her appearance in the parlour, no more time is needed than is necessary to dry her hand. Thus armed there is no danger of being caught, indeed, in this case the catching is apt to be the other way. American females have a sleight of hand in getting through house-work of all kinds without apparent labour.[5]

One of Eliza Julia's talents was her ability to make hard work look easy. Was George's description of the lady of the house who "dresses and adorns herself for the parlour" before beginning the family laundry realistic in a day when water had to be heated in large tubs on the stove or outdoors over an open fire, and bulky clothes had to be rubbed on a washboard and wrung out by hand? It does not seem reasonable, and one can only assume that Eliza Julia protected her husband from the "awful day of an English six weeks wash," which he clearly viewed with dismay. She apparently made even that drudgery appear to be more pleasant than it really was. Given her love and care of her husband, she was probably careful to do heavy tasks when he was not at home.

Although George Flower tried to show his appreciation for his wife's labors, women's roles may be better described by other women. Englishwomen transported to the prairie had to adapt quickly to the American ways and especially to the lack of servants. A letter written by George's sister, Katherine Flower Ronalds, from her home at Hazel Hill makes it appear unlikely, however, that they found the transition as easy as George made it seem. Writing to a younger brother in England, she advised him not to bring his bride to the English Prairie, saying that female servants were becoming even scarcer than they had been earlier. She added,

I have learned to do completely without them. . . . I will give you one of my days: up at daybreak, make the fire, call Kitty, Hugh, Emily [her children]. K. sets breakfast. H. picks up wood and chips for the fire. I begin the occupation appointed for the day which I divide as equally as I can to prevent my doing more than my strength will afford of. One day I wash, 2nd iron, 3rd make soap, 4th candles, 5th bake, 6th clean house. After breakfast K. and H. calculate for about half an hour on Mr. Thequey's machine which brings them forward nicely after which Kitty cleans the breakfast table and puts all the things that have been dirtied the day before into a large tub and it is Emily's business to wash them whilst Kitty (who is quite a capable little body) wipes them and puts them in the right place. Hugh in the meanwhile pulls the weeds in the garden then the children have leave to play till I have done my work, but Kitty generally prefers staying to help me.

Kate went on to say that when her self-assigned work was completed about noon she spent two hours with her children at their lessons while the youngest napped. After lesson time she did the family sewing and tailoring, following the usual pattern of the frontier woman who made all the clothing for her family. In the late afternoon she worked in the garden gathering fruits and vegetables, which she then had to prepare for supper or preserve for later use. The children were fed first and put to bed. Then she says, "Hugh and I sup and chatter, read a little while but are generally too tired to sit up long."[6] The children, Kitty and Hugh, mentioned in this letter as being so helpful to their mother, were six and five years old respectively at the time. Little Emily who washed the large tub full of dishes was just over two and one-half. Since most households were dependent on the help of children, even households where education and culture were considered imperative, it is clear from Kate's letter that children learned to work early.

Although Park House was a mile from the town of Albion, Eliza Julia and her family were not as isolated as many frontier families. On the contrary, their home was a significant social center. For many years Park House, in addition to being hospitable to travelers and visitors, welcomed local families as well. Several weddings, besides those of the family members, were held before the lovely mantelpiece in the drawing room of Park House. In a recently published history of Edwards County, there is an entry in one of the family histories, "Eliza Naylor, born 1813 and Jonathan Briggs (1810–Sept 1833) were married January 31, 1833 on the south porch of Park House." There is no known connection of this name to the Flower family beyond one letter from Kate Ronalds to her mother that Mr. Nailor would return her horse to Park House to be cared for in her absence. He may have been an accommodating neighbor or a hired hand.[7]

Groups such as a debating society met there regularly. On alternate Friday nights a musical evening was held when congenial guests with good voices and musical instruments like the violin and the flute gathered around the grand piano and sang and played. In describing these evenings, Duke said, "Their many visitors were impressed by the beauties of Park House."[8] Eliza Julia wrote in her letter of March 1834 that she "had less leisure than any other woman in this State," perhaps a heavy price to pay for the pleasures of sociability.

Along with her roles as housekeeper, laundress, tailor, and teacher, Eliza Julia often found herself, if not the family doctor, at least its nurse. Caring for the sick was indeed another facet of housework. Keeping healthy was a perennial concern that the Flower family of Park House shared with other families who settled on the Illinois frontier. A major criticism made by many of the detractors of the English Settlement was that it was an unhealthy place in which to live. The settlers wrote back to England denying this charge. Some of the visitors to the English Prairie were sent by emigration societies to learn at first hand the truth of the matter, and some of them were guests at Park House.

In a letter of 2 August 1834 in which she had expressed her pleasure that Charles had decided to come to Albion, Eliza Julia had also written, "We in the open prairie have . . . preserved our health," an important statement for her to have made considering the concern about illness that was prevalent at that time.

Park House near Albion

August 2nd 1834

My dear John,

We are always pleased to recieve a Letter from you and very glad shall we all be to see your brother Charles—I shall write to him by this post at Shawnee Town—as also a few lines to Mr. Docker—requesting him to attend to him there and forward him to us with all speed—When Charles has been with us a short time so that I can form some idea of his Character I shall write to you again and I shall desire Charles to keep up a regular correspondence with you wh. may benifit him and satisfy you as to how he is going on etc.—If Mr. Flower and he should happen to suit each other wh I hope they may—they may and will I have no doubt be a mutual advantage to each other—I observe what you say as to C's. Education—he shall have every advantage wh we can give him—we have a very excellent collection of Books and take several Home and foreign News papers wh I think are very useful to young people as well as older as they give you a summary kind of knowledge of what is going on in the world and sometimes stand you in the stead of much learning. If anything should happen to detain Charles until this letter reaches you—I wish you would send by him ten or fifteen Dollars worth of little trinkets—for the Children and for their young friends—say earring and drops—necklaces Broaches etc.—some of the common most kind that aren't expensive and yet look shewy and gay—I will pay the amount to Charles here or give you a Draft upon Mrs. Flowers Banker at Philadelphia in my next letter. I should like some white wax necklaces in immitation of Pearl for Emma and Ear drops to match—I should also like a very large Broach I care not of what material it is made—for my own turban—I dont wish any varieties of Colour—let it be oval in shape and either Jett or mock Pearl on Gold—I am very sorry for your loss in the Partnership but I hope it may turn out for the best—There is to me something more satisfying in having a business to oneself even if the profits are smaller—I shall like extremely to hear all about you and yours from Charles and I shall wish Charles to describe us all exactly to you—We are all well—on the Wabash Banks and bottoms there is a great deal of sickness but we in the open prairie have hitherto preserved our health wh after all is the greatest blessing we can enjoy—Give my kind love to your Wife and little ones—I have a little son three weeks old last night—my Thirteenth Child and I believe he is the stoutest and finest looking child I have had but a bad baby at night wh makes me feel very tired all day—I shall write of your brother George in my next and of your own prospects after next May—Good night we all unite in love to you all—

I am your truly affec'te Aunt

Eliza J. Flower

When Eliza Julia wrote to her nephew John in November, she described a long trip the Flowers and some friends had taken after an illness of her husband. There is some indication that this trip north was a business trip. We know from other correspondence that in October 1834 George Flower, with a man named Captain James Carter, took a drove of Flower cattle north and was away from Albion for five or six weeks. The time frame would suggest that this was the trip Eliza Julia described in her letter, and if it was, she once again managed to turn even a rigorous cattle drive into a pleasurable journey.

Park House

November 27th 1834

My dear John,

Charles tells me that he has recieved a letter from you by this days Post and altho' I haven't seen the letter I doubt not but that you reproach me for my silence—pray forgive me—I plead guilty as to the fact but not as to the intention of neglect—it would take up this whole sheet if I were to tell you half the causes which prevent my having time to write to anybody—now if I could describe to you all that have to do would you scarcely believe me—Therefore supposing myself forgiven—I must send my kind remembrance to your *better half* and little ones and proceed—Charles and George are both here and well—Charles's manners are extremely against him—I cannot think how or where he acquired them—he is so reserved that I know little more about him than I did when he first arrived—but his conduct is irreproachable—he is steady industrious and obliging—he is at present at the Mill in the day time but sleeps here and takes his meals—we are just returned from a journey of six hundred miles wh we took partly to see a friend—and partly for the recovery of Mr. Flower's health who has had a very severe attack of fever this summer—We travelled a strong party as you shall hear—Mr. Flower on Horseback—Myself Infant boy and daughter Rosamond in a two Horse Waggon driven by Charles your Brother—an ox team to convey the Baggage viz Bedding Provisions and Camping and Cooking utensils—(for in the Wild Country you must provide for yourself lest Providence should fail to provide for you)—an elderly Gent a friend a hired servant and our two eldest Sons—made up our party, and a very pleasant trip we had—the Weather was delightful—the Roads good—we had plenty to eat and drink—excellent appetites!—we cook'd on the Road and Camp'd by night some in the Waggons and some around a huge blazing fire—we all grew most vulgarly fat and Mr. Flower recovered his health—Charles improved a great deal on the journey both in his appearance and manner—and altho he still wants a good deal of *rubbing* up—I cannot help thinking that he is sterlingly good—I always tell him when I see anything in him which I dont like—I treat him exactly as one of my own sons whether he likes it or not—there is no opening at present whereby he can gain money—but I daresay there will be soon—meantime this House is his home and as I told you, I would supply all he needs to the best of my ability—and so I will—and his Uncle is desirous to put him into a business as soon as ever it lies in his power—C. is too backward in writing to you—I often remind him to do so—and it isn't for lack of Love toward you and yours that he does not—for I believe he thinks you the Best Brother and your Wife the very best Woman that this World contains—As to George I hardly know what to say of him—he is certainly a most impudent selfconceited strutting young pickle! Still as he is but young he may come out right at last—I hope he will but what upon earth you thought I could do with him do pray tell me in yr next—, We have placed him in a Merchant store in Albion and he comes down here on Sunday—I hope this Merchant—Mr. Churchill—an Englishman who is a good sensable man—will keep him at present he is there only on trial and we pay for his board at the Tavern in Albion—I think he seems disposed to keep him and if he does I know that he will do Geo justice—I sent Geo to school to improve himself in writing and I *lecture* him when complaints are brought to me against him wh he doesn't like but he has to bear—he has grown very fat and robust bursting out his Cloaths—You needn't feel any uneasiness about either of them—we will do our best for both— tho I certainly feel the most interested for Charles because I think he best deserves it—and now dear John you are the person of all others that I most wish to see here—if you could come and pay us visit next Spring—do you think you can in prudence? and return to your business and family with recruited health for I have no doubt but a journey would be extremely beneficial to your health—Give my kind love to your Wife by the account I hear of her she is worthy of everyones love and doubly so of yours my love to the little ones—tho I have so many Children of my own that I am pretty well tired of the little *torments* be pleased to behave better to me than I have done to you and write to me as soon as you can and tell me all about yourself and your concerns

believe me your Affc'tte Aunt

Eliza J. Flower

Since traveling in a large party for six hundred miles was bound to demand a good deal of closeness on the part of its members, it is in character that Eliza Julia had difficulty understanding how her nephew Charles could be so reserved. Hers was an effervescent outgoing personality. She was sociable and a good conversationalist who loved meeting people, and her children apparently absorbed her attitudes and mannerisms. The family always had large gatherings, and as long as George and Eliza Julia lived, they never missed a wedding, birthday party, holiday, or any family get-together.

She wrote that Charles "needed a good deal of rubbing up." Her view of her role in the family included the education, the discipline, and the polishing—the rubbing up—not only of the immediate family, but also of Charles. It was not George, the father of the family, who had this responsibility, but Eliza Julia, the mother. This assignment of responsibility makes the Flowers a "modern family" in contrast to a "patriarchal family" characteristic of families on the prairies at the time.

Degler and others contrast the roles of women in patriarchal and in modern families. The subordinate roles of the women in the former are replaced in the modern family by special and important functions such as discipline and education, which become the special province of women.

In her letter of 2 August 1834, Eliza Julia had expressed her joy that Charles at last would come to Albion, and she was able to report to John in her letter of 27 November 1834 that he had arrived and that she finds him to be a "sterlingly good" person. It must have been a great surprise for her to also have Charles's brother, George, as an addition to the family. While Charles needed only a little "rubbing-up" to fit into the family, George, being a "most impudent self-conceited strutting young pickle," presented her with serious problems. Charles and his brother George, having been taken into the family, received the same discipline and education as the younger Flowers.

This letter reveals two principal facets of Eliza Julia's character. First, it shows her love and concern for her husband at the expense of her own needs and health. She did not mention that she was probably near exhaustion, caring for George during his illness as well as for a new baby so soon after her own confinement. She did note that the baby was bad at night, which made her feel tired all day. Second, it illustrates her remarkable ability and imagination to see the romantic and the beautiful in any situation.

Eliza Julia's description of a journey of six hundred miles taken partly for her husband's convalescence from a fever would not have seemed unusual to her nephew. It was common practice for the English to travel either during or after an illness. The trip she described may have been undertaken for a combination of reasons: the long-standing cultural habit of the English for restorative sea voyages and the relief derived from being away from the hardships of pioneer life and the responsibilities of daily living. In any case, there is much evidence in the letters of the settlers that such a remedy worked. Many nineteenth-century Americans also traveled, and for some of the same reasons that stimulated the Flowers. Eliza Julia had always liked to travel. Long before her emigration to America she had traveled extensively through England and Scotland and visited on the Continent on at least two occasions.[9]

Maintaining their health was one of the problems all immigrants faced. Despite some reports of sickness on the English Prairie, it was known as one of the healthiest places on the frontier. Its favorable reputation was no accident. Neither of its founders, Flower and Birkbeck, liked forests, and both noted in their writings the gloom and dampness of heavy forestation in Ohio and Indiana. They also commented on the dangers of the river banks and bottoms. It was accepted frontier knowledge that river lowlands were feverish. They chose their site deliberately and very well, halfway between the Wabash River and the Little Wabash River on the highest plateau between the two, which made it a healthy place. In addition to this favorable location, the English settlers, because of their agricultural background, had a good diet, a varied meat supply of lamb, pork, beef, and fowl, and many health-promoting garden vegetables. Both the Birkbeck and Flower farms included dairy cattle for milk and cheese. Sound housing may also have played a part in the unusually healthy state of the English settlers. The houses often featured stone foundations, heavy wooden floors, and chimneys and hearths constructed of brick. Such careful construction made the houses free of chill and damp.

In spite of every precaution, however, the new settler on the frontier was apt to experience a "temporary indisposition." In one of his *Letters*, Birkbeck stated,

Change of climate and situation will produce temporary indisposition, but with prompt and judicious treatment, which is happily of the most simple kind, the complaints to which new comers are liable are seldom dangerous or difficult to overcome, provided due regard has been had to salubrity in the choice of their settle, and to diet and accommodation after their arrival.[10]

Illinois, in general, had a reputation for being unhealthy owing to the prevalence of a type of malaria that tormented its victims with fevers and chills and, although it did not kill many of them, tended to recur with depressing regularity. More serious illnesses—milk sickness, typhoid, tuberculosis, and smallpox—were also common. Richard J. Jensen describes the illnesses of the time in some detail,

Illinois was considered very unhealthy. New arrivals could soon expect to fall sick, and many died before they were fully established. The crude housing might have offered protection from Carolina winters, but it was inadequate for Illinois. Hundreds died in the bitter winter of 1830–31. The settlers suffered from frequent exposure, a lack of hygiene, unbalanced diets, a rudimentary knowledge of healing skills, and endemic malaria. In large stretches of the new land, as late as the 1840s, virtually everyone was infected with malaria, or ague. The disease followed a curious course. In the fall just before harvest time, one or more family members began showing symptoms—fever, violent shakes, chills; the next day the patient would feel normal, and the symptoms appeared again on alternate days. Quinine was known to help, but it was too scarce and expensive for most sufferers. Usually the ague spells would cease in a few days, to recur the following year or perhaps skip a year before striking again. The disease was seldom fatal, though its debilitating effects could weaken a person enough for other diseases to kill him. The best opinion held that poisonous vapors, especially along river bottoms, caused ague. Not until most swampland had been drained and the mosquito menace curbed did scientists discover the true cause.[11]

Robert Howard wrote, "On the rugged frontier, those who survived were a hardy breed,"[12] a good description of the Flowers. After the "seasoning" of the first year, the English settlers kept remarkably healthy.[13] Medical proficiency, good hygiene, and the careful choice of a site ensured the health of the English immigrants in spite of such primitive conditions as the lack of sewage systems and the prevalence of vermin, houseflies, and the ubiquitous mosquito.

A stone house in Albion. One of two early houses built by Richard
Flower for the town, never occupied by the family, but illustrative of solid
housing. Courtesy of the Illinois State Historical Library

The first inhabitants of Albion were fortunate to have a capable medical man, Dr. Charles Pugsley, as physician. He had come from London in 1818 among the earliest settlers. Traveler-author William N. Blane wrote that

one of the principal inducements to settle at Albion, in preference to any other place in the state is, that there is a very clever English surgeon there who having had a regular education under Abernathy, and walked the hospitals in London, must be a great acquisition to families in the neighborhood.[14]

Unfortunately, Charles Pugsley was also a troublemaker who caused so many problems in Albion that the Flowers were delighted when he left for Nashville in 1825. Dr. Archibald Spring began to serve the medical needs of the community in 1821. His father, Thomas, had brought his family from Derbyshire, England, to Albion in 1820. When Dr. Spring joined the family the next year after completing his medical education in Baltimore, he became a practicing physician in Albion. He and Dr. Pugsley were bitter enemies until Pugsley left. Dr. Spring practiced in Albion for thirty years and for a long time was the only doctor there.

Fred Gustorf wrote in 1835 of health and sickness and attempts to alleviate the latter in Albion.

In Joel Churchill's store, where the clerk also serves as pharmacist, they sell quinine, calomel, castor oil, laudanum, and camphor dissolved in alcohol to the sick in great quantities. The doctors (the local doctor is named [Archibald] Spring) are not as well trained as German physicians. They ride around the country visiting patients on horseback. Very often the patient will send an emissary to Doctor Spring to ask what can be done. When riding horseback the doctors carry medicine in a leather bag, which they throw over the saddle. With the aforementioned drugs the doctors cure all diseases. The doctor feels the pulse with a significant expression on his face, then opens his bag and shakes a certain amount of medicine on a little piece of paper. This procedure is repeated with every patient—Albion, which is sixteen miles from the great Wabash, is healthier than the western counties.[15]

In addition to the diseases like the ague that the frontier people had to cope with, there were also the problems of accidents. There seems to be a letter missing in which Eliza

Julia told John about an accident that had happened to his brother Charles. Apparently, his elbow had been broken and had not healed properly. Eliza Julia took him to New Harmony for consultation with the surgeon there. The first reference to Charles's accident appears in a letter some weeks after the event.

Harmony Indiana

April 27th 1835

My dear John,

I wrote to you some weeks since concerning Charles's accident wh letter I hope you have recieved since that time his Elbow instead of getting better got worse—and two weeks ago I took him to Harmony for change of scene and for more advise upon having the arm particularly examined by the surgeons here—they are of the opinion that the bone is not now at all properly set—and that Charles must undergo the operation of having it *reset* or lose the use of his arm probably for life—this is a very serious thing for a young man—and the whole concern has been a source of extreme trouble and anxiety to me for my own family is so large and my Husbands health so delicate that it is almost impossible for me to give Charles the attention he requires and now to that I find the bone is not set nothing that I can do will be of any use to him—His own great wish is to go to Cincinnati to an eminent Surgeon there—but as he cannot work or do anything even for his board it will of course be a considerable expense—ever since he has been with us—we have made him as one of our own Children—tho we have had nothing for him to do one quarter of the time even whilst he was in health and now for 3 months I have nursed him and we have a heavy doctors bill to pay on his account—all this he is welcome to and more if we had it to spare but with our large family we have not. George has been a very heavy expense and I have just got him off our hands—George is a vain carless fellow—and—has no feeling as to what expense and trouble he gives any one—I must say that I have felt him a great burthen—I went three separate times to Mr. Churchill, his Master before I could get him to take him and pay anything even his board and he came to me with literally the one Black Suit upon his back and a few very old Cloaths in a Handkerchief—so I was obliged to get him new summer clouths directly and he was so careless about his Black ones wh were good that he soon tore them up to rags—and complained that they were too small for him—this Winter I have again supply'd him with warm good plain cloaths a good Great Coat shoes etc— and now since March 1st Mr. Churchill gives him 50 dollars a year and pays for his board at the Tavern therefore I consider that I have done with him and tho I do not believe by the way he goes on that he will make the $50 hold out—Yet I shall not do any more for him and this I have informed him—Yes—I still pay his Washing and Mending—because I think that he ought to have a little Pocket money—lest he should ever feel tempted to touch what doesn't belong to him and in a general Store that is a great temptation

for 7 months Board at 1.50 --------$42		This is what I
Great Coat----------------------------$12		have paid for
Doctors Bill------------------------------4		him George
Other clothing as per store bill-----10		
$68		

Now dear John this account I should not have sent to you if I had plenty of money to spare—But I really do not know how to afford it for this boy—who came quite unexpectedly upon me and at a time too when it was particularly inconvenient—you may be very thankful that you have got rid of him—for if we can hardly manage him *here* where almost all boys and girls do well—Trouble enough you wd. have had with him in the City for he will scrape acquaintance with every one good or bad and has no judgement or discretion in his friends—I do not ask you to pay these expenses of George's—but I wish you to know what they have been—I think it is very likely that he has written you a swaggering letter about himself—but *I tell* you the truth—at the same time I am pleased to tell you that since his Master has paid for him he has made him work much more and he is more steady and industrious than he was and I still hope that he will do well—He has remarkably grown and very improved in his appearance and so has Chas.

About poor Chas. I feel differently—we invited him here—he has always behaved well—he has been particularly careful to put us to as little expense as possible—my Children all love him—and so do I and everything that I can do for him I will do—but I cannot make money—therefore this is what I am going to propose to you and that with Chas. consent—viz—That if you will advance $100 for Chas. to pay his expenses of Board and Doctor etc. at

Cincinatti until he gets well again—that Chas. will repay you out of his wages as soon as ever he is able to work and what he cannot pay you I will—I think dear John that this is not asking too much from a kind brother like you—and I hope you will be able and willing to do it—the Mode of sending the money to me or Chas. I propose to be this—either a hundred dollar note in a letter wh wd arrive safe or to pay one hundred dollars into Warders and Brother Philadelphia to the account of Mrs. Eliz'th Flower of Albion and then she can draw a Bill to that amount for me and I can get it cash'd directly at either of our stores at Albion—Send me an answer by return of post—I must send Charles directly for every day makes it worse and worse for his poor arm—my kind love to your Wife and the little ones—in haste dear John, I am

Your affectionate Aunt

Eliza Julia Flower

Almost from the beginning of the English Settlement, from the first family illness when George credited her with saving his life, Eliza Julia's reputation as a good nurse grew. She frequently cared for the sick and injured in the settlement. In 1826, when George was making his way back to Nashoba she saved his life again. He became critically ill while crossing the Ohio River en route to his destination in Tennessee. He later wrote to his brother,

On returning [to Nashoba] again I was seized with a violent bilious fever on the banks of the Ohio about twenty miles below Shawneetown where I lay at the point of death for many days. I was afterwards removed to Shawneetown where I am recovering and hope in a week to be well enough to go down with my dear family in a steamboat.[16]

There were many instances in which Eliza Julia proved her competence in nursing skills, but resetting a broken bone in an arm required medical expertise beyond her abilities. She provided nursing care for her nephew Charles when he needed it, but he had to leave Albion for professional medical attention.

The Flower family members were a hardy breed; they did survive, and Eliza Julia was more than the inspiration for their good health. Considering the work involved in raising all her children, her continual struggles to maintain the health of the family, and in addition the physical and social demands placed on her by Park House, Eliza Julia showed that she was a woman of many talents and great stamina. When George wrote of her "sleight of hand in getting through house-work of all kinds without apparent labour," he attempted to show his appreciation, if not his full understanding, that his wife's work was never done.

Chapter 6

"The business of the merchants is very extensive."

James Stuart

WHEN IT WAS CLEAR that Charles's arm could not be
properly treated in Albion, he was sent back to his brother
John in New York. Eliza Julia's letter of 15 October tells us
how much both she and others missed him. She also wrote
that she had had the full responsibility for running the
Flower estates for at least a month while George was away.

Park House

Oct. 15th 1835

Thursday Evening

My dear John,
    Your letter which I recieved some weeks ago—gave us great
relief as well as pain—relief that Charles has reach'd you in
safety—and pain to think that the poor dear fellow should have
had more suffering to undergo—and no benifit from it!—I'm sure
he must hate the remembrance of this place since his visit to it
brought such sorrow to him—beg Chas. to write to me when he
has really settled something with Mr. Clark—I wont hear of any
excuse about "can't write" I know he can write and much to the
purpose too therefore give my kind love to him and tell him I can
take no excuse!—I am rejoiced to hear of your improved health
and the health of your dear Wife and Children—long may it
continue—we have had much sickness in our part of the country
tho not much in our family—Rosamond has had a severe attack of
intermitting fever from which she is now recovering—Your Uncle

and Alfred are gone to Ohio to purchase 1000 sheep to add to our present flock—they have been gone 4 weeks and *Camilus* and *I* and *Mary* and *William* are all shepards and thus far we have done very well—Tho I long for my dear Husbands return—tell Chas. Mrs. Waterman has been staying 3 weeks with us and sends her kind respects to him—Anne Coad is married to a long legged Yorkshire man 7 feet high! Albion stands much as it did—the old Mill *is still* Willie Wood has return'd from England—much as he went only with some bags of money tack'd to him—John Wood his brother is putting up a Castor Oil Press in conjunction with Mr. Harris Mrs. Hearsum who used to keep Mr. Hank's House—had become a widow and shortly after married old Mr. Wood in the Prairie!—Children born without end and some few deaths but not many—Miss Burkett has return'd to England—Sally Hall *not married* Mrs. Mary Hale of Harmony quite in love with Charles! Old Mr. Rogers and Daughter been staying here both send their love to Chas! in short Chas. was a favorite—Dear John I often feel sorry that I could do no more for Chas. but I couldn't—we have such a large family and such an expensive Household as Chas. can tell you—that I work very hard to keep things together and that Chas. can tell you also—It gives me great pleasure to speak of George—I think I may say that he is in every way improved and I now confidently hope that he will make a useful and respectable man—he is very often with us and his Cousins and he are very happy together—I lend him a horse whenever I have one to spare on Sundays for him to take a ride wh is a great pleasure to him— sometimes Emma rides with him sometimes the boy, sometimes he rides alone—he grows stout and healthy—and is much improved in his person—I am not sure if he will stay with Mr. Churchill when his time is out (for Mr. Churchill talks of giving up the store)—and if he should not he wishes to bind himself for 4 years to a useful trade wh I quite approve of for a Mechanic in this Country is perfectly independant—but I shall write to you if any change takes place and enquire your wishes—I consider George as one of my Children and as such I shall advise reprove or commend him as I see necessary—and if he is wise he will recieve it as I intend it—from affection to him—Give my love to your father and mother I always intend to write to them—but *time time* I have none—and we have had our house full of company since Chas. left us—and during the Harvest we were from 25 to thirty in family! so I'll leave you to guess what time I have for writing—My kind love to your better half and the little ones— believe me

yr affc'tte Aunt

Eliza J. Flower

Twenty-five to thirty in family was a lot of company to care for at any time. As long as the Flowers lived in the house there were always visitors. Years later, George Flower wrote about the many people who came to their house: "I think there must have been something original in our settlement, to attract so many tourists of original and eccentric character, both men and women as it did. To portray them all faithfully would take a volume in itself."[1]

Old Park House, near Albion, would long be remembered by old settlers and distant visitors for its social reunions and openhanded hospitality—strangers and visitors to the settlement received a hearty welcome, saw all there was to see, and received all the information they wished for, with necessary refreshment and repose. It may truly be said that, for thirty years, Park House was never without its visitors, from every country in Europe and every state in the Union. They were welcome, unless the family was absent, if their stay was for a week, a month, or a year.[2]

The work involved in caring for all these visitors must have been endless. It is no wonder that Eliza Julia moaned, "Time, time, I have none." Rarely does one find evidence of Eliza Julia being anything but courageous and indefatigable. However, Kate Ronalds, her sister-in-law, wrote to her brother in England in 1839, noting that people had changed in that year more than any other year in the history of the settlement, "so many people have grown old, even Mrs. George has added at least 10 years—lost her spirit and her beauty."[3]

It is impossible to know the extent of Eliza Julia's "beauty" when she was fifty years old, but it is clear from later developments that her spirit certainly bounced back.

When he arrived in the English Settlement, Charles worked with George Flower in his enterprises, which could have meant in a grist mill, pottery kiln, or cotton gin or on the land. Eliza Julia felt he had other options, too. By 1834, there were mechanics established in Albion for almost any agricultural or village need: blacksmiths, carpenters, masons, potters, tanners, weavers, shoemakers, nurserymen, and millers, any of whom might have provided employment or an apprenticeship for Charles. Several new businesses had been established. George Flower had started one of the first stores in the settlement, which he later turned over to his cousin, Elias Pym Fordham. There were soon at least two more stores, one operated by Moses Smith, the other by Gibson Harris. Harris had first come to Albion as the manager of a store for a Vincennes proprietor but later went into business for himself. Although Eliza Julia wrote to John that Albion stood much as it had, business increased in Albion and the county seat became the hub of local trade.

The story of Joel Churchill is illustrative of the success of a local businessman. Joel Churchill was an educated man from London and Exeter who had traveled extensively in Europe, Africa, and Asia. He was the son of a prominent Quaker clothier who had a turn for business. Churchill did an extensive business over a large area for some years. In May 1830 James Stuart, a Scotsman, traveling by carriage visited the settlement and commented about Churchill. "Mr. Churchill, one of the storekeepers, is principally engaged in raising the castor oil plant and making the oil on an extensive scale."[4]

The Churchill oil presses had been purchased from Cincinnati and transported to the English Prairie at a total cost of $3,000, a substantial sum in those days. They weighed several tons and were said to have sunk a boat on the Wabash when being transported. Edgar Dukes, author of *Yesteryears*, states that "a hundred years ago, Albion was far-famed for its castor oil, for Churchill was a thorough and careful chemist, having a reputation for making the best and purest brand of castor oil on the market."[5]

Churchill built a brick store on the public square and developed it into one of the most successful establishments in the area. He had a reputation for being a character, since when he moved to Albion from the southernmost part of the English Prairie he brought his pet wolf with him. He also had a reputation for kindness, both as a merchant and as a postmaster. He held the latter position for many years.

Eliza Julia, who found her nephew, George, to be something of a problem, placed him with Churchill to learn the merchant trade. Since his residence, however, was a two-room stone addition behind the store, and not ample for boarders, George Andrews had to be boarded by the Flowers at the nearby hotel. Churchill did not give up the store as Eliza Julia feared, but the arrangement with him for her nephew did come to an end.

Other merchants included Eliza Julia's brother-in-law Hugh Ronalds, who very early shipped as much as 200,000 pounds of salted pork to New Orleans. By 1836, pork had risen to $5 per hundredweight. George Flower took the wool from his sheep to the New Orleans market. Albion became much more self-sufficient, virtually a regional trading center. Businesses in the community expanded. John Tribe had a carding mill; Elias Weaver, a German potter who left Harmonie in 1825 for Albion, was the first potter in the village. By 1831, George Bower from Bavaria was making good pottery in Albion.[6] Tinsmiths provided all the needed pots and pans. There were several stores in addition to Churchill's and two good hotels. Stuart noted that the town was substantially built with a broad main street in the English manner, and that

the business of the merchants is very extensive. They buy up the produce of the land, consisting of wheat, maize and other grain, of cattle, salted pork, butter, cheese, and other articles, which they carry to New Orleans and there they purchase sugar, coffee, tea, foreign wine, woollen cloths, and all those articles which the Illinois planters require for their own use.[7]

Merchants in Illinois and elsewhere in the Midwest were essential elements in the development of the towns where they lived and worked. In addition to buying and selling, they served as bankers, promoters of agriculture, and developers of markets for agricultural crops. Their services made possible an orderly transition from a pioneer stage of life—a self-sufficient economy—to an interdependent economic specialization—an advanced economic order. Their contribution to the settlement of the Midwest, although sometimes overlooked, was significant.[8]

As Albion grew and changed, English settlers continued to find their way to the English Prairie. A second wave of immigration came, arising from the private correspondence of the first poor men who came, who having done well themselves wrote home of their successes.

After the easing of the hardships of the first twenty years, the people could give more attention to visiting and amusement. Hunting for sport rather than exclusively for subsistence was popular; deer, prairie hens, and turkeys abounded on the prairie.[9] Eliza Julia liked to ride to hounds, and was said to be an excellent shot.[10] Fishing in the Little Wabash River was good sport, and all-day visits, parties, and frolics occurred in abundance.

Life in Albion had many benefits, and most of its people were friendly, but the problems of buying and selling goods and services were ever present. The absence of cash was a constant problem. Stuart's description of Albion merchants differs somewhat from the views of the historian and former governor Thomas Ford, who wrote about Illinois in general, not Albion specifically:

Commerce from 1818 to 1830 made but a small progress. Steamboats commenced running the western waters in 1816, and by the year 1830, there were one or two small ones running on the Illinois river as far up as Peoria, and sometimes further. The old keel-boat navigation had been disused; but as yet there was so little trade as not to call for many steamboats to supply their place. The merchants of the villages, few in number at first, were mere retailers of dry-goods and groceries; they purchased and shipped abroad none of the productions of the country, except a few skins, hides and furs, and a little tallow and beeswax. They were sustained in this kind of business by the influx of immigrants, whose money being paid out in the country for grain, stock and labor, furnished the means of trade. The merchant himself rarely attempted a barter business, and never paid cash for anything but his goods. There was no class of men who devoted themselves to the business of buying and selling, and of making exchanges of the productions at home, or those of other States and countries. The great majority, in fact nearly all the merchants, were mere bloodsuckers, men who with a very little capital, a small stock of goods, and with ideas of business not broader than their ribbands, not deeper than their colors, sold for money down, or on a credit for cash which when received they sent out of the country.[11]

The problem of cash, or lack of it, led to the demand for banking facilities, but banks were not well developed for many years. Shawneetown, one of the oldest settlements in

Illinois, housed the land office for southeastern Illinois and had the first bank in the Territory of Illinois, established late in 1816. In 1834 the legislature chartered a new state bank with six branches, one of which was to be at Shawneetown.

The Mr. Docker Eliza Julia referred to in her letter of 23 April 1833 was Thomas Docker of Shawneetown, a merchant who served as the local agent for the Flower family. He did not, at least in the eyes of the Flowers, fit the characterization Ford assigned to men of his work, although there were undoubtedly some who did. His kinsman W. A. Docker was a director of the Shawneetown bank.[12] Thomas's correspondence with Frederick Rapp, business manager of the Harmonist Society, on 10 May 1823, offering his services to be the Rappite commission agent in Shawneetown, gives some indication of his character. He said that he had been accustomed to the mercantile business from the days when he was a schoolboy both in England and in America. He indicated that he was well established in Shawneetown for selling goods and told Rapp, "I flatter myself I could give you every satisfaction in the disposal of your productions and in the general routine of your other business."

Gentleman that he was, he added that should the Rapps consider continuing their business with the widow of their late agent, "I at once decline my proposition as I would on no account interfere with her welfare."[13]

A letter in November of that same year indicates that Docker did not get this commission, but as a merchant he continued doing business with the Harmonists.[14]

Lacking what Eliza Julia called the "portable dollar." the Flower family used the services of several agents to conduct business for them. In addition to Docker, their other principal agent was Jeremiah Warder, a Quaker in Philadelphia. Warder, working with agents like Docker along the river, made it possible for business to be conducted between the populous East and the sparsely settled West. Through these men arrangements were made for shipments of supplies sent to the settlers, guests were directed to the English Prairie, and produce from the settlement was sent to distant markets. Warder was not only their business contact in the East and in England, he was also their friend. A letter written by Warder to George Flower's brother in England, now preserved in the Chicago Historical Society library, is an excellent example of the friend-businessman relationship of the parties and the variety of business they transacted.

Philadelphia

11 mo. 19th 1827

We wrote thee on 9 mo. 22 to the care of John Greaves, Barford, near Warwick with certificate of 81 shares upon the bank of the United States which at the market value amounted to $15,028/75, transferred to thee by order of thy father—Our last notes from him are of the 14 and 25th-ulto when it appears his health was restored. We have never heard of W. Pickering whether he remain in England or has returned home by New Orleans, we know not.—Six months since thy father sent us a box of plate to be forwarded to thee, but have been unable to meet with a suitable private conveyance. We now ship the same on board the ship Montezuma consigned to Martineau, Smith and Co to whom we enclose bill of lading. The box we have had covered with canvass and contains . . . .

After listing the contents of the box, Warder goes on to give Edward financial information regarding the state of the market for bank shares, the current price, and the exchange rate.[15] Acting as agent for Richard Flower, Warder transferred eighty-one shares of United States Bank stock, discussed the whereabouts of a family member, and explained in detail how he packed and shipped valuable family silver sent by the father to his son, Edward. Clearly, the functions of the agents were myriad: stockbrokers, bankers, purchasing agents, shippers, and confidants. It is no wonder the rather isolated settlers depended upon them so heavily for help with their financial affairs.

The last letter in the correspondence between Eliza Julia and John Rutt Andrews was written nearly sixteen months after its predecessor in response to an inquiry from John about the absence of news from Albion.

Park House

February 2nd 1837

My dear John,

I this day recieved your letter of the 16th January—and truly grieved am I—that my negligence should have caused you and your poor Mother pain—I recieved your letter of Sept, and every day intended answering it but every day brings me more work than any *mortal* can get thro—and every night I go to bed more tired than a Slave—But to the point of your letter—George is in Cincinati doing extremely well—earning $5 per week with a prospect of its being doubled in a short time if he continues industrious and steady—I sent him there to a particular friend of ours—where I knew that both his morals and his health would be attended to and where I knew that he would have a vigilent tho' just *Master*—for George as you know requires a Master's eye and advice—George improved extremely both in person and character before he left us—and it was because I saw no chance for his advancement in this small place—that I procured him the Situation he is now in at Cincinati—I sent him nicely cloth'd with money in his Pocket—a good introduction—a Cabin Passenger in the Steam Boat in short—he had every chance that ever any one of my own Sons will ever have and I hear that he is very much respected—I assure you dear John that he was more anxiety to me that any of my own Children—and tho I often *Scolded* him—I guarded him with a Mother's care and love—and George will tell you the same—George's old Master Mr. Churchill gave him an excellent character for truth and uprightness and said that he never saw any lad improve so much as he did in the last six months that he was with him but Geo—and Mrs. Churchill couldn't agree—therefore G had to leave! and all things considered it was well! Geo is fond of ease and company—he was very often with us here—This is a large kind of open House full of Company and variety—not a good place for a young Chap to lounge in if he has his bread to get—G was very respectful and attentive to me—but the Elder Children and he couldn't always agree and G. must always be Master!—Now as I never allow of any tyranny in this house and your Uncle and myself never exercise it ourselves and as I wished the Cousins all to live in harmony and Geo was in every point as my Son—if they couldn't agree—then the wisest way is always to separate before any enmity takes place—and now my dear John you know all about George—I love the boy—I often hear of him I often send messages

to him his Uncle called upon him last August when he was at
Cincinati selling his wool—but I have no time to write anybody or
I should have written to you long long ago—Give my kind love to
your dear Mother and father I will write to them and I will *if
possible* write to George and desire him to answer your letter—
perhaps you didn't get his right address—Mr. G R A at Mr. Wm
Orange Merchant Cincinati Ohio—I haven't written to dear
Charles tho he has written a very nice letter to me—I love Chas
dearly and I believe Chas loves us all tho he is a *Budge Concern!* I
will write if possible but Oh John if I was to attempt to describe
one tenth of what I have every day to do and think of—you *would
not believe me!* Your Uncle is President of a certain Rail Road wh is
to run thro this Town—He has been in Vandalia the Seat of
Government in the State—the whole of this winter during the
Sitting of the Legislature—and most likely will not return home
until the breaking up of the Houses—Meantime I am Master,
Mistress, Servant—in short *Factotum*—the Children are very useful
but they are only Children—Your Cousin Emma is *Married and
gone*—She is very happily married and we all love her Husband
very much—he is a fine young fellow perfectly of her own
choosing—a Merchant by profession—and doing extremely well in
business—Emma is a very captivating Girl and makes a pattern
Wife! so much for a Mother's vanity—they live in Albion—they
very often come down to see us—but I seldom or ever have time
to go and see them—We have a very large farm—a large flock of
sheep a quantity of Horse Hogs and Cattle—all to be fed and
attended to—our House is always full of Company—and I am
consequently a Slave!—Give my kind love to your dear Wife—I
did truly sympathize with you in the loss of your little Babe—and
trust that the other dear Children will be spared to you both! how
I long to give a peep at you in New York!—someday I think I
shall—Give my love to Charles if you ever see him poor fellow
how is his arm? Good night my dear John—or rather good
morning! for it is now 2 oclock—and I must be up by break of day!
I have already written a very long letter to your Uncle since
Supper—he expects to hear from me by every mail—or he is
miserable!—he dearly loves his home—and dearly I love him and
dearly he loves me and this separation is almost more than either
of us can bear! be sure you let your Father and Mother know all
about George—Geo wrote me that he had a long letter from his
Parents some time ago—and told me he should write to them—*I
make no promises* but depend upon it that I wili endeavor to write
to them and to Chas—I am always rejoiced to hear from you—my
Children all unite in kind love to yourself and your Wife and

Children—I have five as fine Boys as ever you saw—and two as smart girls coming up!—I wish we could shew each other our Children—for you know that "every Mother think her Bobby better than another"! I am

your Affc'tte Aunt

Eliza Julia Flower

Reading her reply, in which she listed some of the demands placed upon her as "Master, Mistress, Servant, in short, Factotum" of Park House, one does not wonder that she was "more tired than a slave." George was no help at Park House because he was in Vandalia lobbying for the railroad. Vandalia was, at that time, not only the capital of the state but also the western terminus of the National Road. Emma married in 1836, and although she was living in Albion not far away, she was not readily available to assist her mother. Among the children remaining at home to help, several were small and required Eliza Julia's care and concern. Much of this letter reports to John about his brother George, who had moved on to Cincinnati after maturing under Churchill's and Eliza Julia's tutelage. In it one can again read that Eliza Julia is that "modern woman" whose work includes raising, educating, and disciplining children, as well as managing Park House. Eliza Julia's "modern" attitude is also revealed in her willingness to permit her daughter Emma to marry a man of her own choosing, since in the more traditional practice the choice of a suitable husband would have been made by the parents.

William Orange, the merchant in Cincinnati to whom Eliza Julia had sent her nephew George, was an 1818 immigrant to the English Prairie and an old friend of the family. He joined a brother, Daniel, in his home called Orange Grove, about a mile south of the Flower property on the English Prairie. The Oranges were descendants of a French Huguenot family. Their great-grandparents had left France secretly for England to escape the Catholic persecution, and like their great-grandparents, they had left their country for a better life in a new land.[16] William Orange was a skilled worker in brass and bronze, a trade of no use in Albion. Looking for a livelihood, he was licensed in 1824 to keep a hotel and vend spirits and did in fact keep the Washington Inn in Albion for about a year before becoming a merchant. A few years later he moved to Cincinnati, where he entered into business. Sometime after that the Orange family returned to Illinois and built an excellent house, where they lived until the time of the Civil War.

The railroad Eliza Julia mentioned was the Mt. Carmel–Alton line, which was to extend across Illinois from the Mississippi River to connect with the line being built from Louisville, Kentucky, to Vincennes, Indiana. The charter of the road had been granted by the legislature in 1836, a year before her letter was written. A company was formed, of which George Flower was president. George describes the railroad in his history of the settlement.

The road was afterwards relinquished to the State, and known as the Southern Cross Railroad. The State of Illinois, after expending three or four hundred thousand dollars, sold out all of its interest in this, as well as every other state work. That state interest was bought by Gen. William Pickering, through whose exertions a new company was formed, uniting the two companies into one under the title of the Alton, Mt. Carmel and New Albany Railroad. I was president of the Illinois company for its first three years. When the work was commenced by the State a heavy expenditure was made near Albion, on a deep cut—This road for three years gave me a considerable expenditure of time and money.[17]

William Pickering was a brother-in-law of Eliza Julia, having married George's sister Martha. Pickering, always a promoter, accumulated a large amount of land, served a number of years in the Illinois Legislature, and later, as a friend of Abraham Lincoln's, was appointed governor of the Washington Territory.

Railroads represented a tangible expression of the early Illinois settlers' desire for internal improvements. Internal improvements meant transportation for farm products to markets. The Ohio and Mississippi rivers had served as the great water routes to St. Louis and New Orleans, but the return trip upstream was tedious and dangerous. Steamboats had

trip upstream was tedious and dangerous. Steamboats had come up the Wabash River as far as Terre Haute as early as 1823, and in 1850, steamers stopped in Peoria 1,286 times.[18] Transport by steamboat also had its hazards, such as shifting sand bars and other navigational problems that could disrupt shipping schedules. As late as 1843, the General Assembly of the state of Illinois asked its representatives in the Congress of the United States

to procure the passage of an Act providing for the removal of obstructions in the navigation of the Western Rivers, either by means of snag boats or otherwise, as to the wisdom of Congress shall seem best calculated, to secure an object of the highest importance to the people of this and other Western States and territories.[19]

Transportation by water was important to the development of Illinois. In the beginning, the Ohio and Mississippi rivers were the major routes of transportation. When the Erie Canal opened in 1825, it provided a broad avenue between northern Illinois and the East, so that in 1833 the town of Chicago was growing rapidly; this new canal made it possible to send goods to New York instead of to New Orleans. The new artery of transport also brought floods of immigrants to the West. By 1836, those who wanted to sell land to immigrants and those who had farm products to sell or items they wanted to buy more cheaply coalesced to persuade the state of Illinois that it was in the public interest to build more roads, more canals, and more railroads, all of which were called internal improvements. Railroads began to replace waterways as the more popular routes of transportation. However, the construction of railroads required great public expense. The legislature voted more than ten million dollars for improvements, which included roads, canals, and railroads, plus some money for consolation to those counties that would have no public improvements. Ford further writes, perhaps a little bitterly,

It is very obvious now that great errors were committed. It was utterly improbable that the great number of public officers and agents for the faithful prosecution of so extensive and cumbrous a system, could be found in the State.[20]

Each community along a proposed rail line wanted the work to begin there. To all this confusion was added the general depression of 1837, which caused the state of Illinois to stop all work by 1839 and to sell off the projects to private investors like Pickering and Flower, who were no more successful than the state had been in furthering internal improvements.

Undoubtedly some of the many visitors to Park House who contributed to Eliza Julia's busy schedule were George's railroad associates. Certainly George's extended absences put more responsibility on her shoulders. His expenditures for the railroad and the open hospitality he required contributed to the financial problems that would soon plague the Flowers.

George Flower experienced financial problems after his mother's death that were hard on him and especially on Eliza Julia, since she had to become the breadwinner of the family and to cope with creditors and bill collectors. Two letters written in 1844 concerning settling the debts of her son-in-law, Hugh Pentacost, provide an example of stress and of hurt but also of her ability to prevail. It was unusual for a woman of her time to be so competent in business affairs. George Flower had gone East to purchase a thousand sheep for two men from New York, a transaction for which he would be paid $200 and expenses for his expert judgment. He had his son Camillus with him. Eliza Julia was living in Grayville at the time and in late June received a letter from a merchant in New Harmony demanding payment in thirty days and ending with a threat. The letter arrived while Eliza Julia was ill with the ague. She responded with an eloquent letter in which she explained that George was out of town, what he was doing, and told the merchant that he would have money upon George's return. She said she was expecting him home momentarily, and ended her letter,

I am sorry you closed your letter with *a threat!*—To us who have suffered so much, and still must suffer—who have given up Park House and all we possess 'til every security debt is satisfied

To me who am now supporting my family in a small tavern in Grayville by the very "sweat of my brow"

To my children who have one and all given up their home,
their birthright—the haunts of their infancy and all their sweetest
recollections (To *them* the "loveliest spot on the Face of the
Earth")—without a murmur or reproach—rather than their father's
name should be sullied, or his heart grieved—to such a family
was it necessary was it kindly to remind them they are yet in your
power?—I think that your better feelings will answer for me!
When I read your letter to my children and explained to them the
meaning of the last clause and they all exclaimed "Let all go if it
must be so—we can and will all work". Then I felt that poverty
had lost its sting—for God Tempers the Wind to the shorn lamb

Very Respectfully,

Eliza Julia Flower[21]

Her signature, firm, precise, legible, and oversized, described
well the depth of her feelings.

Eliza Julia was angry, but her eloquence did not end the
matter. A month later, having received a letter from her husband, she wrote again to the creditor, Nettleton. Still angry,
she explained that although George had undertaken this trip
specifically to get the money to pay the merchant's security
bill, because he had been held up by untoward events and
because George would not be paid until the sheep were all
delivered to their destination, they had made other arrangements to pay immediately. Wool had been sold and a draft
could be paid on demand. She then continued in a very practical manner to tell the creditor just how she proposed to go
about it. She said she would draw a draft in Nettleton's favor
on Lawrence and Co., Boston, and hand deliver it to Mr.
Mayo, the respected county clerk of Edwards County, who
would then hand it to Nettleton. She explained that the
Pentacost judgment was in Edwards County and had to be
settled there. She wrote,

This I hope will answer your purpose. I have been looking for Mr.
Flower from day to day—and find by his letter that he has met
with many untoward events in the purchase of the sheep which I
believe I mentioned in my letter to you was the object of his
journey to the East. It was expressly to pay you that he has taken
this journey, and as he will not recieve the money until the sheep
are delivered at their destination—he gives you a draft upon Mr.

Lawrence who has just received advise from me that the wool is shipped for Boston and will honor the draft at sight.[22]

George Flower owed $211.72 on the judgment against his son-in-law, Pentacost, so the $200 commission he was to receive for selecting the sheep would have just about paid the debt. Five days later, Eliza Julia added a postscript reporting that she had written to Mayo at Albion sending him Nettleton's receipts. She went on to suggest that the merchant could send his attorney or authority to her and that she would write a draft in her husband's name as he had authorized her to do for the full amount, or if he preferred to wait, on George's return he would ride over to New Harmony and hand Nettleton the draft or cash himself. She ended her letter by writing that she was extremely mortified that the money was not paid by the twenty-fourth (a month earlier), which Nettleton had specified and she had promised. She closed her letter, "the events which detained Mr. Flower were beyond his control."[23] Staving off creditors was not easy, but Eliza Julia did it well.

The economic conditions affecting the English Settlement were more negative than one would believe at first view of the story, or from reading contemporary accounts. Birkbeck and Richard Flower, as well as the many travelers who passed through, were enthusiastic about the prospects open to immigrants to the Illinois Prairie. Birkbeck and the Flowers not only invested a great deal of money in making their original down payments on land in Edwards County but also pledged themselves to pay the balance in the next four years. Birkbeck expected to sell some of his land to the immigrants who followed them, and the Flowers expected to develop a lucrative wool market selling their farm products to markets such as those at New Orleans. They both expected to make profits from their work. When they failed to do so, much of the land they had contracted to purchase reverted to the government.

In 1817, when they arrived in Illinois, there were many good signs that their hopes would be fulfilled. European crop failures, for example, opened markets for American farmers. But by 1820, there was a general economic panic that dashed

Photograph of a letter signed by Eliza Julia Flower showing her signature. Courtesy of the Illinois State Historical Library

their hopes. This recession caught them and many others by surprise.

In this mode [on credit], by the year 1820, nearly the whole people were irrecoverably involved in debt. The banks in Ohio and Kentucky broke, one after the other, leaving the people of those states covered with indebtedness, and without the means of extrication. The banks at home and in St. Louis ceased business. The great tide of immigrants from abroad which had been looked for by everyone failed to come. Real estate was unsaleable; the lands purchased of the United States were unpaid for, and likely to be forfeited. Bank notes had driven out specie, and when these notes became worthless, there was no money of any description left in the country—The people began to sue one another for their debts; and there was absolutely no money in the country, it was evident that scarcely any amount of property would pay the indebtedness.[24]

In 1820, the state of Illinois was persuaded to charter private banks like the ones at Shawneetown and Edwardsville that would issue paper money, making gold or silver coin (specie) unnecessary for business transactions. When these banks failed, the state created a state bank in 1821 to issue paper that was to be accepted to pay debts.

At first it [the value of state paper] fell twenty-five cents, then fifty, and then seventy cents below par. And as the bills of the Ohio and Kentucky banks had driven all other money out of the State, so this new issue effectually kept it out. Such a total absence was there of silver coins, that it became utterly impossible in the course of trade, to make small change. The people from necessity, were compelled to cut the new bills into two pieces, so as to make two halves of a dollar. This again further aided to keep out even the smallest silver coins, for the people must know that good money is a very proud thing, and will not circulate, stay or go where bad money is treated with as much respect as the good. For about four years there was no other kind of money but this uncurrent State bank paper.[25]

By 1825, the state bank had collapsed, and the notes had to be redeemed by the legislature. In 1832, President Andrew Jackson closed the United States Bank and encouraged states to create their own. In spite of the difficulties of the 1820s the state of Illinois again chartered a state bank. This unwise decision was a part of the overly ambitious internal improvements programs. The national economic panic of 1837 exacerbated local problems in Illinois. The state stopped paying interest in 1841. The financial picture could hardly have been more gloomy. Money that had been invested in banks was now worthless. If a farmer planned to buy stock or seeds in the spring, he could not get a loan, and if a man attempted to collect from a debtor, he received devalued paper or nothing at all.

Much of Richard Flower's money had been expended over the years for the improvement of Albion: courthouse, market house, library, hotel, mills, and bridges all for the good of the immigrants. The panic of 1837 did not immediately reach the English Prairie, but that year, in her last letter to her nephew, Eliza Julia again alluded to the costliness of maintaining Park House and its traditions of hospitality, and she referred to the curtailment of their income caused by George's inability to sell his wool in Louisville, his usual market. Incredibly, the lavish hospitality of Park House continued as ever, long after it could no longer be afforded.

The final blow to the Flower fortunes was the failure of the United States Bank in which Elizabeth Flower had placed the bulk of her money. She was left with barely enough to live on. George Flower was in such desperate straits by 1842 that he offered much of his mother's Park House estate in mortgage to try to obtain working capital for his farming operations. He wrote to Attorney Joseph Wead, Royston, Hertfordshire, England,

Dear Sir

My long absence from England, has left me but few correspondants indeed my exchange of letters is now limited to my Brother. As the business upon which I desire information is almost necessarily connected with your proffession I address this letter to you professionally, as well as upon the score of former acquaintance. The limits of half a sheet require the utmost brevity. My Mother has sustained a loss of all her money in the U. S. Bank, when that institution failed. No personal inconvenience has yet occur'd to her in consequence I am happy to say, as my farm supplies her household with meat, Bread—vegetables fruits and fuel. A small amount of money yet preserved to her in the rent of two houses—allows her to keep her servants & furnish her clothing.

You know the disasters and discredit that has since overtaken almost every State in the Union. Illinois two Banks, viz the "Bank of Illinois at Shawneetown" & the State "Bank of Illinois" These institutions furnished 5,000,000 of Dollars circulation. They have failed. From these and other causes the utmost pecuniary difficulty prevails. Thus the act of prudence (in keeping some *money* in what was considered the best institution in the Country) has been the source to us of some difficulty. Banks when they fail here do not die an instant death as with you, but linger long, their paper getting lower & lower. From the causes above stated I am left almost without a dollar, but in possession of a handsome property, of 16000 acres of land on which I reside, town property, a valuable flock of fine wooled sheep &ct &ct. I owe as principal and security to these two Banks 5000 dollars Their paper has depreciated one half, & had I any good dollars to command by the purchase of their paper my liabilities would be actually reduced by one half. It may be asked why not sell some property, simply because there is *no* money to buy with at this time. These extraordinary monetary revulsions have overtaken us like a thief in the night. I am desirous of preserving my valuable property & not have it sacrificed to a broken bank.

I wish to borrow L 1500 upon a part or even the whole of my property and would consent to give (if needs be) 5 per Cent for the same if the interest is made payable in England, or 6 per Cent if the interest is payable in America. I say annually because the sale of the fleeces of my fine wooled flock would be the fund for the interest.

As interest is so low in England, I apply to *you* and to my *Brother* to whom I have also written to know if you can find the sum I have named to be loaned on landed Security.[26]

In spite of their very best efforts, the economic tides ran against the Flowers, and also many other of the early settlers, as Miller indicates:

The builders of towns in southeastern Illinois were beset by all or most of these environmental, political, and economic problems, but they fought hardest against the difficulties of a financial character. One might escape floods, diseases, and county seat wars for years, but one never gained respite from the effects of restricted markets, labor shortages, inadequate means of transport, lack of money, poor credit facilities and business cycles.[27]

The timing of the settlement of the English Prairie could not have been worse.

Chapter 7

"[George Flower had] the unwaning love of a high-minded warm-hearted, spirited woman."

Robert Dale Owen

$\mathbf{P}$ ATTERNS OF ECONOMIC MISFORTUNE continued to follow George and Eliza Julia to the ends of their lives. They attempted alternatives to farming with diminishing success. Family financial problems were central to their difficulties, but these were outweighed by the devotion of the parents to each other, their devotion to their children, which was reciprocated, and the affection of the children for each other.

George was not fortunate in the turns of the business cycles and was not as practical or as capable a manager of finances as his wife. The construction of buildings, roads, and bridges in Albion were investments that Richard and George had made for the development of the community. The construction and maintenance of Park House were also great expenses. He had idealistically spent much of his money on his altruistic projects, spending hundreds of dollars to send slaves to Haiti and much more to finance the venture with Fanny Wright at Nashoba, where they had planned to educate freed blacks. Both projects had taken much of his time and money, as well as some of his father's funds, draining his reservoir of cash in hand. Although he owned many acres of land in Illinois, he was land-poor because he lacked enough hard money with which to hire labor at a time when few men were willing to work for others.

Lawsuits brought against them were also expensive. Although the judgments eventually were largely settled in favor of the Flowers, before 1825 the family was obliged to spend a great deal of time and money in court fighting the numerous lawsuits filed against them, lawsuits that had been precipitated for the most part by their role as founders, colony leaders, and money lenders. Yet George never lost his philanthropic spirit. At the same time that George was trying to obtain a mortgage on Park House and the land, he and Eliza Julia made a gift of a city lot in Albion for St. John's Episcopal Church, the cornerstone of which was laid 2 September 1842.

George Flower's mother, Elizabeth, died in 1846, four years after most of her money was lost in the failure of the United States Bank. For the next few years George struggled to halt the erosion of the remains of the once considerable family fortune. Even the difficulties of their children's endeavors worked against them. In 1836 their daughter Emma had married, as Eliza Julia first described him, "the successful young merchant, Hugh Pentacost." Unfortunately this young man was not as successful in business as Eliza Julia had supposed he would be when she first wrote to John about Emma's marriage. Pentacost's Albion store had proved to be a complete financial disaster, and because George had gone security for this son-in-law, his own financial problems were compounded, as evidenced by the dunning Nettleton letters in 1844. The Pentacosts moved to New Harmony, where they hoped to be more successful. In 1849, George and Eliza Julia with their youngest son, Benjamin, made a trip to New Harmony intending to pay a six-month visit to their eldest daughter and her family. When they arrived they found to their horror that once again Emma and Hugh were in desperate financial straits. Eliza Julia decided that the young couple should move to Evansville, Indiana. In this nearby rapidly growing Ohio River town she thought Emma could establish a boarding house while Hugh took a job training as a riverboat pilot. George and Eliza Julia remained in New Harmony to pick up the pieces. Eventually George and Eliza Julia paid all of Hugh Pentacost's debts in New Harmony.

Their long visit in New Harmony may have allowed George a respite from the last few years of disheartening business frustrations and time to contemplate plans to recoup his losses. Since George did not have enough capital to continue to farm his large holdings, he and Eliza Julia decided to take over the Pentacost property and run it as a hotel. This property was a large brick structure originally built by the Rappite colony as a dormitory. Park House, near Albion, was left in the care of their eldest son, Alfred, then twenty-three, and the Flowers became innkeepers in New Harmony.

Once before, when Eliza Julia needed to become a bread-winner to supplement the family income, she had turned to the occupation she knew best: that of homemaker and gracious hostess. In the 1840s she had briefly kept a boarding house in Grayville, a town just south of the English Prairie. Now, in New Harmony, she turned again to that occupation in earnest to earn most of the livelihood of the family.

The United States Census of 1850 for Posey County, Indiana, shows George Flower, age sixty-four, described as an innkeeper, living with his wife Eliza, daughter Mary, and sons Richard and Benjamin in dwelling #320, the Community Building of which Flower House was a part.[1] George had purchased the property for the Pentacosts. When they left New Harmony for Evansville, he felt obligated to spend the last of his capital to refurbish and furnish the hotel in order to make it a comfortable inn called "Flower House." Eliza Julia ran the inn with the help of her children. She had not misled John Andrews when she wrote that her children were brought up to work, were not afraid of hard labor, and were expected to do what their parents asked of them. Mary, nineteen, very willing but not as physically strong as Eliza Julia, was indispensable to her mother in running the hotel. Young Benjamin, fourteen, was responsible for cleaning the guest rooms. Richard, the baby Eliza Julia had described earlier in a letter to John when he was three weeks old as the "stoutest and best looking of all, but a bad baby at night," at fifteen took complete responsibility for the horses and the stable.

George was left to garden and write. Being unable by habit and deafness to contribute much to the operation of the

The Rappite Dormitory No. 2, New Harmony, Indiana, used by Eliza
Julia and George Flower when they were reduced to innkeeping.
Contemporary photo by Lewis G. Hall, Jr.

hotel, George felt that gardening was the least he could do, for with fresh vegetables he could provide the hotel with a well-set table. After a stint in the vegetable patch each morning, he spent the remainder of his day in writing the *History of the English Settlement.* He had undertaken this project at the request of the recently formed Chicago Historical Society.[2]

George also wrote business letters in attempts to recoup some money. In February 1860 he wrote to an unknown attorney seeking help, telling him that William Pickering had mortgaged the Mt. Carmel-to-Alton Railroad and asking if the roadbed could be attached. He explained in detail how the railroad company was set up, but confessed he had no money and asked the lawyer to take the case on a contingency basis. George said that he would send the attorney the necessary documents if he agreed to take the case.[3]

Eliza Julia made the best of the situation and became the perfect hostess for their New Harmony Flower House. In 1851, fewer than two years after they began to operate the hotel, she was described by Robert Dale Owen, a contemporary.

Let me begin with the Flowers who keep the principal tavern in the place; and a most comfortable, tidy, home-atmosphered sort of house it is. They emigrated from England some thirty years ago, wealthy farmers on a large scale. Mr. Flower having won, for several successive years the highest prize for the best Merino sheep in England: prizes which still appear on his tavern table, in the shape of handsome pieces of plate. He brought with him ideas of an improved system of agriculture inconsistent with the then state of the country; run through much of his property in unsuccessful attempts to introduce expensive improvements; lost many thousands of dollars by going security for an idle, worthless, dissipated son-in-law and finally the family having thirty-thousand dollars invested in the U.S. bank stock, lost the whole by the failure of that institution. Throughout all of these reverses George Flower never lost the open hearted, generous spirit of a hospitable English gentleman. He kept almost open house long after he could ill afford it. And for a long term of years, there was not a stranger visiting Albion (the name of the settlement he made in Illinois, about 25 miles west of this) who was not invited to make his house—beautifully situated on the edge of a lovely prairie—his home, so long as he saw fit to stay.

Chiefly to pay his security debts, one piece of property after another went, at a ruinous sacrifice. And at last, after a long struggle to save it, the favorite homestead, too, went with the rest. The sole remaining consolation was, that by such sacrifices he paid up every debt he owed to the world, and stood, at last, a free though landless man. I ought not say the *only* consolation, for he had one which might well support a man under worse reverses than these; the unwaning love of a high-minded warm-hearted, spirited woman. Mrs. Flower is quite a character. Even now, at sixty, or near it, the mother of six or seven children, all of adult age, after a life of continued labour, and renewed disappointment, she retains the vivacity and almost the cheerfulness, of early youth. To the remains of great beauty, she still joins a raciness of wit and a sprightliness of fancy, which make the life of any society in which she happens to be. I am sure she will amuse and interest you, you must expect to see an extraordinary looking woman; a somewhat short figure inclining to embonpoint, not bent with age, though the hair is silvered; an aquiline nose and Eastern looking face; the head often surmounted by a most voluminous and uncommon looking turban, with lace depending from its folds. Altogether a figure and character anything but commonplace. She took to the toils of tavern keeping for a living—and you know what they are in a country like this— without a murmur. It was not a great deal more labour or trouble, she said to me one day, than to keep open house at "Park Place", as she had been used to do: the only difference which grated on her feelings was the making out these odious bills and demanding so many dollars and cents from each guest before they departed. Amid all the cares of the tavern which sometimes fall on her without any help whatever, she preserves her spirit unbroken, and still finds time for a thousand touching little attentions to her husband, helpless rather from habit than age, and in part from a degree of deafness which renders an ear-trumpet indispensable. She usually has with her their youngest daughter, Mary Flower, with a face as pretty as her name, and a disposition corresponding to both. Mary, with her bright eyes and her real auburn hair and her 19 or 20 years, is an excellent true hearted girl without much literary cultivation but devoted to her Father and Mother, inheriting a spark of her Mother's spirit, but unluckily not her Mother's bodily strength, or she could more effectively assist her household cares. A married son, good like the rest of the family but somewhat rough in his exterior, with a pleasant girl for a wife, has lately been added to the household.

They have a large commodious dwelling, rent free; and I believe they are making an humble but comfortable living. The family have maintained their honor and integrity unblemished, through all reverses, and are in consequence treated with every respect, now in their fallen fortunes. I often spend an agreeable evening with them.[4]

Another view of Eliza Julia during this period appears in a newspaper clipping in the collection at the Workingmen's Institute in New Harmony, probably from the *New Harmony Times*. The author of the undated article interviewed Julius Miller, a New Harmony resident, who in his description of Eliza Julia also recounted the sad story of a robbery.

Mrs. Flower was fashioned after the *grande dame* type and insisted that everything about the hotel be strictly formal. One of the strongest rules she observed was that every man entering the dining room wear his coat and a number of instances are on record of guests going without their dinner because they had left their coat at home.

When the Flowers came to New Harmony they were in greatly reduced circumstances. Their chief asset was the family plate amounting to several thousand dollars which was kept in a heavy chest, securely locked. One night burglars entered the house, forced the chest and carried away the entire collection of plate. It was the crowning stroke of misfortune to a career that had not been particularly successful. After this the Flowers removed to Mt. Vernon where they ran a hotel for several years.[5]

Some time during 1855 or early 1856, George and Eliza Julia left New Harmony for Mt. Vernon, Indiana. They had lost the family equity in Flower House when the [state-appointed] administrator of the McClure estate, A. P. Hovey, repossessed the building along with other properties originally belonging to William McClure. The Community Building, which had served as Flower House, belonged at one time to McClure, a partner of Robert Owen in the early years of New Harmony. After a quarrel, McClure and Owen divided the town along the line of Church Street, now Indiana Highway 66. McClure took all the property north of this line, which included the large Community Building, shortly after which he moved away. McClure's property was managed first by Madame Fretageot, then by Thomas Say, and finally by McClure's brother, Alexander. When William McClure died in 1840, although Alexander had as his legal inheritance only a sum of money, he and his sister, Anna, took their brother's property and disposed of it freely. A decade later, when Alexander died, the state of Indiana, aware that his actions were not in keeping with William's will, appointed A. P. Hovey, who instituted a number of lawsuits to regain control of McClure's former holdings. He then resold them at much higher prices, and the money was used as McClure had intended, to create libraries, Workingmen's Institutes, throughout the country. The McClure case was discussed in *The Advocate* of Mt. Vernon on March 30, 1855, and it was reported that Hovey dispossessed many in New Harmony to regain the money that he believed should be in the estate.

The amount involved will probably exceed $200,000, most of which will ultimately be expended to establish libraries for the use of such as earn their livelihood by the sweat of their brow.[6]

On the 4th of June, 1856, lot #2, the Community Building (Flower House), was sold to James Sampson and A. E. Fretageot.[7] Three years later, Sampson sold his share to Fretageot. It was just before the first sale that George and Eliza Julia were dispossessed and decided to leave New Harmony.

The census of 1860 reports "George Flower, age 74, male gardiner, living with his wife Eliza Julia at Mt. Vernon, Indiana, on lot #174, a property valued at $700."[8] The designation as gardener would seem to indicate that George continued to provide fresh vegetables for the tavern table in Mt. Vernon as he had in New Harmony.

In the autumn of 1856, the Flowers were visited in Mt. Vernon by George's nephew Charles and his wife Sarah from Stratford-upon-Avon, England. Charles was the son of Edward Fordham Flower, George's brother, who had returned to England in the 1820s. Sarah wrote in her diary,

Charles' Uncle George looked quite venerable with long white hair and handsome features but being very deaf made him appear very old. [George was 68 years old at the time of this visit in 1856, and Eliza Julia was 64.] Mrs. Flower looked very stylish in the turban which she had always worn, having brought the fashion from England, most becoming it was![9]

Sarah went on to say that Richard, Mary, and Ben were all still at home with their parents and gave their visitors a hearty welcome. Eliza Julia and Mary were actively engaged in the operation of the Mt. Vernon Flower House, but were yet able to be so hospitable that they were described by Sarah as "actively entertaining, gay, lively and sociable." Eliza Julia was still a good hostess and had not lost her vivacity. Sarah thought they had a "busy, hard life" but mentioned that they hoped soon to retire from the hotel business and move to a small house.

In April 1858 Eliza Julia wrote to her son Camillus after a visit with him and his family on the English Prairie, where he was still farming.

Flower House

Sunday April 4th 1858

My dear Camillus,

Mary [Eliza Julia's daughter] didn't get your letter enclosing *Thirty Dollars* until *yesterday* Mr. DeSouch [?] forgot all about and had it in his pocket until then! Mary thanks you kindly it came most acceptably

I am rejoiced dear Edith [Camillus's wife] is better I hope she will continue to mend with her four beautiful boys she cannot afford to be sick besides the misery of it! Oh the wretchedness of being sick all the time I would far rather die at once if I Cd choose but I suppose "whatever is is Best"!

I am very sorry our New York Tribune is come to an end because the story of "Debit and Credit" has not—as it regards you and Edith We felt we could not afford to renew it this year for ourselves—but Richard [Eliza Julia's son] and Mary take it and Mary will send you what you have missed of that beautiful story in the Tribune as soon as she has read it herself and her husband only about 3 or 4 Tribunes and then it ends

"Queen Delhi" is much improved but she is not at all strong your Father rides her every day and so would I if I was in the Prairie where nobody would see how awkward I was with my

Portrait of Eliza Julia Flower, courtesy of the Patricia Flower Martin
Collection

lame arms and weak back She is gentle as a lamb and just shedding her coat your Father has grown quite fond of her—but Richard will never ride on her—to be sure he has got his own beautiful Nag I call him "Arabian" Hes a beauty and as gentle but young and frisky!—I rode out behind him last week Richard driving me—and tho' I half expected to have my Neck Broke every ten minute with his friskings and jerkings about—still I enjoyed my ride very much I was so glad to get into the air and I so admired the *"Creature"* I am going to make a large black Nett to cover him all over in "fly time"

Emma [Eliza Julia's daughter] is coming here as you know Mary is going to Housekeeping Mary hopes and prays that Joe Wood will be ready with his wool money within a *month* for McArthur [Mary's husband] has got $400 out of the Bank last week but now must renew in 30 days instead of 40 days as Richard thought he could As soon as Emma gets here I am going to Rosamond [Eliza Julia's daughter] for a short visit and to you and Edith and Alfred [Eliza Julia's son] and Lizzy [Alfred's wife] just to see you all if I can hold out my strength I think the change may strengthen me I seem to want the air so much Not one word from William [Eliza Julia's son] any more than if he were dead and buried I wish he would marry some kind good girl and settle down in his own home and not live the forlorn life of an old Bachalor any longer I have written him 3 long letters not one of which has he answer'd and since then just before I was taken down this last time your Father wrote him a sweet kind letter Still no answer! tho he writes to an old comrade and friend who went with him to California but returned to live at Harmony He writes to him by every mail

I shall write once more when I feel my spirits and strength equal to it it distresses me that he should behave so He was always a kind gentle Boy at home but I believe that low company and absence from his relatives has changed his character—disappointment too, chiefly of his own seeking has added Still he is my own child and I love him

goodbye dear children—both of you all love to all the little Brood I want to see the Babe I often think of you all—My kind love to Alfred, Lizzie & Children dear Camillus

I am your affec Mother

Eliza Julia Flower[10]

This letter, written more than twenty years after her letters to her nephew, clearly confirms much about Eliza Julia's love for her family as was revealed in her earlier letters to John Andrews. Money problems had haunted the Flower family for some time, but by 1858 they overshadowed most of their lives. They had to cut expenses so sharply that they could no longer afford to take the New York newspaper, a seemingly minor expense compared to their former lavish expenditures at Park House on the prairie.

One important change in Eliza Julia's life is notable in her description of herself. At age sixty-six, Eliza Julia had begun to lose her formidable strength and for once admitted to weakness, which kept her from riding horseback in public and doing other things that she had been accustomed to and really wished to do again. She had been very ill in late 1857 and for the first time it was an illness that caused her family to feel concerned.

A letter to Camillus from Benjamin in January 1858 said, "Mama is much better," and about the same time her daughter Mary wrote to Camillus and commented on her anxiety about her mother. She wrote,

The last few days she has improved very much. She gets up every day to have her bed made, sits up for an hour or more. Today she ate quite a good dinner. I think she is getting along very well now, better than at one time I ever thought she could.[11]

There seems no doubt that she had been quite ill and no doubt that her spirits were depressed by William's estrangement. The only one of her eight living children who was not in her immediate sphere, he had gone to the California gold fields and had not kept in touch with his mother. It was difficult for her to bear that he wrote to a companion who had returned to New Harmony rather than to her. Despite her distress, however, she remembered the "kind gentle boy" and expressed her love for him. Eliza Julia could be hurt by her children but never angry at them.

Mt. Vernon records show that on 26 July 1858, John T. Mayor and his wife sold lot #197 in the Owen Enlargement to George Flower.[12] The 1860 census lists Richard Flower and his wife, ages twenty-six and twenty-one respectively, as hotel keeper living at dwelling #73, a property valued at $1,600, which must have been the Mt. Vernon Flower House.[13] The property George and Eliza Julia bought from the Mayors was near the Ohio River. Ironically, this property has now been washed away by the strong and capricious currents of the Ohio River. That this should happen is no surprise to those who live along the banks of major rivers and experience spring flooding. In February 1859 Eliza Julia's daughter Mary, writing to her sister-in-law on the English Prairie, reported,

> We have had such incessant rains that the river has come up higher than it has been for many years. It is up under the balcony of Ma's house. If it rises one foot more they will have to empty their sellers. I am very glad they are home now so they can attend to it.[14]

Perhaps floating away down the Ohio River was a fitting end to the last piece of property owned by the man who of himself said,

> It is an historical fact that the discoverer of new countries and the first founders of settlements in new countries, rarely attain any material advantages—wherever prudence greatly prevails as an element of character no explorers or first founders of settlements will be found.[15]

After George and Eliza Julia had left the running of the Mt. Vernon Flower House to young Richard, they lived in their own small cottage. During this time, they made more frequent and more extended visits to their sons' homes on the English Prairie and to their daughter Rosamond's house in Grayville, where all of Eliza Julia's children and grandchildren often gathered.

For several years George continued writing and revising his history of the settlement in Edwards County. He was assisted by the writings and memories of other first settlers who were still living. As soon as George had finished the history of the settlement in which he and his family had played such an important part, William Barry, secretary of the Chicago Historical Society, asked him to write a history of

Harmony and the Rappites. Flower's correspondence with Barry and with the Rappites in Pennsylvania shows him to be alert and very interested in the project for which he wrote many pages before his death.[16]

At the end of February 1859, Eliza Julia, apparently unsure whether it was a leap year and consequently dating her letter the 28th or 29th, wrote the last letter that has been found, adding March 1 to the dateline. In many ways it is the most human and appealing of all of them. Having just returned from a visit to their home, she wrote to Camillus and his wife, Edith.

Cottage   Sunday February 28 or 29th or March 1st

Mount Vernon *1859*

MY dear Camillus and Edith

We got home in safety after rather an unpleasant voyage—Bad weather, many stopages on the way for freight—Grand Chain some difficulty—poor company—and "Total Eclipse of the Moon" just as landed between 4 and 5 in the morning *Pitch dark* and pouring with rain I took the greatest care of the turkey so did your Father and delivered him safely to Mary who was delighted and full of admiration She has written to you herself I believe our little cottage lookid very pretty and is very comfortabley—and altho the waters are fully as high as they have been for years it hasn't yet reached our cellars yet—but soon will Yr Father came home just in time to save the new fence of the New garden at "Flower House"—Richard said it was of no use to him he shouldn't garden—we might have it and welcome—if we would look to it and haul it away— so your Father made it safe on the high land and when the roads will permit we shall haul it home and put it up temporally till better times—it will do very and make us much more snug and safe than we are now

I have at last (after a good deal of talking with him) got Richards desire to sell his Land if he can get *$800* for it *in Cash*— that is *$360* clear after paying $40 that will be due in May for interest upon the $400 he has already recieved so if Mr Hardwick or anybody else buy it for *that sum* (or more of course if you can get it)—but dont refuse the $800—and get it as soon as you can so that he may pay Mary up for she is very anxious indeed that her husband should pay up his debts and release the names of those

Front and rear views of a medallion holding a picture of Eliza Julia Flower. On the reverse, a lock of her hair. Courtesy of William Fordham Flower, Larchmont, New York

who were so kind as to go his Security! I believe he has met his
first payment to Dr. Newman—I don't know the particulars—but by
the extremely frugal economical way in which they live & their
dread of incuring debts even ever so small makes me feel sure
that if he has his health—he will get thru honorably and well—*and
make money!*—Rich'd debt to Mary of $400 is due 1st April, and he
has paid nothing on it yet—indeed I feel very uneasy about him
and his affairs altogether—he sees how he stands—and will bear
talking to better than he did—Poor fellow—he has a heavy drag
upon him in his own household—I don't know how it will end
Sell his land if you anyhow can then if he will sell his Horse and
Buggy—and pay the proceeds away where he owes it *directly and
not spend it* in fooleries I think he might straighten himself—I don't
believe he will be ready with the $150 he will owe us in July—so
your Father and I shall save every dollar we get in order to meet
that note or part of it if needs be—Young George sent your Father
$20 last week—wh he immediately put into gold and lock'd it up
in the cabinet *till call'd for!* and whenever the money comes from
Rosamonds Lots—we will take the greatest care of it till we see
how Richard gets thru *July* Your Father and I often talk over the
pleasant [time] we spent with you both—and hope we shall spend
it over again next year—and tho yr Father is very fond of this little
place and so am I—yet both of us have a great hankering to live
nearer to *Grayville and the Prairies* So we shall make this place as
pretty and salable as we can this summer to invite the Eye—and
without spending but little money upon it—and then if should
get a good offer for it in the fall—and can find a small place near
Grayville on your side—I should like to sell *this* and buy *that*—So
you keep on the lookout for us and let us know Your ham is a
delightful one we are very choice of it—I made one of your shirts
before I came home and left it with Rosamond—and have made
the other since I got home (I thought the hog who tore open my
bag in Mr. Williams warehouse and eat up a large plumb cake had
also torn up your shirt with some other things—but fortunately its
snout didn't reach up so high in the bag—and the shirt was saved
to my great satisfaction!

Edith dear—I have made them exactly as you cut them out but
if I might advise—I wouldn't have them *double* in the *front* for
summer shirt—they will be unbearably *Hot* and then too you will
save nothing for I think the perspiration will rot *thru the double*
quite as soon as the single and then too they will be so awfully
heavy to *wash*—think of all these things and then do as you think
best—I should put a *double back* because there is a great strain
upon the Back

I see I have doubled my paper wrong so I have mark'd the pages—Excuse the blunder. I should line the Back of the Shirt with a thiner piece than the shirt itself—it will last quite as long and be cooler.

I do hope you will contrive to pay us a visit this summer. I will make you comfortable and you shall do just as you like in my house—just as I did in yours: and then I know we shall enjoy ourselves.

Rosamond says in a letter to Mary yesterday—"I suppose Alfred is with you?"—No indeed we have neither heard or seen him as yet but I suppose he is on the road and we shall see him when his Holy Mission at Carmi is ended. When either of you write be sure and tell me all about your folks in the far distance! particularly about Alice? & give my kind love to all the bless'd children—good dear little souls they are! tell them if they will build a little room for Grandpa and me close by your New House when you build then I will furnish it all comfortable—and come a month with them every year and mend and make all their cloaths? Goodbye dear Children Write when you feel like it and be sure and come when you can

I am Yr Affec tte Mother

Eliza Julia Flower[17]

Eliza Julia's last letter is a testament to her continuing love and concern for her family. That it may seem unduly preoccupied with money and business concerns reflects the seemingly unending financial upheavals that she and George had been forced to face. Although she remained involved in her children's business affairs and was a never-ending source of advice and even financial assistance if necessary, it was the closeness of the family that was central to her thoughts.

Another illustration of this closeness of the family is shown by the story of the transport of the turkey from Camillus to Mary by way of George and Eliza Julia. Mary wrote her thanks to Camillus for the huge bird on 27 February 1859,

Ma and Pa reached home all safe and well and brought us a most beautiful turkey from you for which we send you both a thousand thanks for it is the greatest beauty I ever saw, I am sure I shall make such a pet of him we shall hate to kill him.[18]

Eliza Julia seemed to have gathered to herself her children's mates as she had earlier accepted her nephews as her own children, as shown by her rather gentle way of pointing out to her daughter-in-law the better way to make her husband's shirts. The closeness of the family was strong enough to allow for her subtle sarcasm when she speaks of her son Alfred.

Alfred had become a clergyman, a founder and minister of the Christian Church in Albion, not the romantic soldier or sailor envisioned by his mother when she wrote about him to her nephew John. Family tales hint that George, and especially Eliza Julia, were not terribly keen that Alfred had become a leader in a branch of the Baptist Church led by the Evangelist Reverend Alexander Campbell. Perhaps Eliza Julia would have preferred him to have been an adventurer on the high seas. When her daughter Rosamond inquired if Alfred was in Mt. Vernon with them, she commented that she had not heard from Alfred and said, "I suppose he is on the road and we shall see him when his Holy Mission at Carmi is ended!"

Eliza Julia wanted most of all to be closer to her family near Grayville and the prairie. "Father is very fond of this place," she wrote, "and so am I but both of us have a great hankering to live nearer Grayville and the Prairies." Characteristically, she had worked out a plan to accomplish this: they would improve their cottage, but without spending much money, they would then sell it at a profit and find a home on the English Prairie nearer their children. Rosamond, her second daughter, had married Charles Agniel, a successful lumber merchant who had built a comfortable home in Grayville. The family gathered there frequently.

That the children were also close to each other and enjoyed being together is seen in Mary's letter written in February 1859 to her sister-in-law on the prairie,

We want very much to meet the first of April in Grayville to see you all. Becky and I wish to start first, then in about a week Mc A [Mary's husband] will come for us. It has been so long since I was up on the Prairie.[19]

Becky is Rebecca McArthur Flower, wife of Eliza Julia's son Richard.

Eliza Julia had trained her children well, for not only were they emotionally close, but following their parents' example they were prone to help one another financially and in other supportive ways. Between 1858 and 1861 Benjamin sought the approval and help of his older brother, Camillus, in a scheme to buy hogs to fatten for market on available distillery slops.[20] Mary asked her brother Camillus to collect a debt for her.[21] Mary and her husband loaned $400 to her brother Richard, of the foolish extravagant ways.[22] Camillus, on at least two occasions, had attempted to sell land for his brother Richard, and as late as 1861 Richard thanked Camillus for taking care of a note for him.[23] Richard's penmanship and spelling seem to indicate that he was the least educated of Eliza Julia's children. He was still in need of money and wanted to sell land. He wrote, "I should like to sell it if I could for money is not very plentfull here. I wan five hundred dollars for it."[24] It was a rare letter in which one family member was not thanking another for some kind of farm produce, a turkey, or a ham.

Eliza Julia's health was not as robust the last two years of her life as it had been earlier, and her remarkable spirit had finally been broken by her son William's desertion, followed closely by the untimely deaths of her two youngest sons. The youngest, Ben, had died in August 1859, when he was just twenty-five years old. Richard, soon after having written to Camillus in October 1861 about selling his fifty acres of land, volunteered as a sergeant for the Indiana Cavalry at Mt. Vernon. Leaving his young wife, Becky, with a small baby, he was sent immediately to his first engagement at Frederickstown, Missouri, where he was killed in a bloody border raid against Jeff Thompson, "the Swamp Fox of the Confederacy."[25]

After Richard's death in the late autumn of 1861, Eliza Julia quickly faded. At Rosamond's home in Grayville on 15 January 1862 both George and Eliza Julia died, she in the morning and he toward evening. They were laid to rest side by side at Oak Grove Cemetery at Grayville. They had wanted to be buried in Albion, but the January weather and poor road conditions made that impossible.

In February 1862 the word of their deaths was received in England, prompting Sarah Flower to write in her diary,

> Heard of the death of Mrs. George Flower and on the same day a few hours after of Mr. Flower. It seems so happy that they should both go together, so dependent and fond of each other as they were.[26]

The lifelong love affair of Eliza and her husband was apparent to all who knew them, even young relatives from England who had known them only on brief visits.

After World War II, their original tombstones were moved to the lawn in front of the Edwards County Historical Society in Albion. New stones, provided by a descendant, now stand in the Grayville cemetery.

The historian E. B. Washburne, in his preface to George Flower's *History of the English Settlement*, wrote, "George Flower was no ordinary man. He has left the impress of his character and his services upon the State, and his name will always be honorably associated with the colony he helped to found."[27]

From her letters and those of her contemporaries an indelible picture of Eliza Julia appears. In a biographical sketch printed in *The Combined History of Edwards, Lawrence and Wabash Counties* one reads,

> Among the pioneers of Edwards County, no one is held in dearer esteem, because of excellent qualities of head and heart, than Mrs. George Flower. . . . Although all her surroundings were so different from those to which she had been in in earlier years accustomed, she maintained her light-heartedness, and to her, more than any other is due the reputation acquired by Park Hall for its hospitality.[28]

In the same volume, as a portion of the biography of George Flower, Eliza Julia is delineated as follows,

> She was of the best type of an English country woman and preserved to the end of her days, the characteristics of her nationality. With her high shell comb and her tasteful turban, no weary guest will ever forget her cheery welcome, or the satisfactory and kindly manner in which he was entertained. All

The tombstones of George and Eliza Julia Flower, modern-day stones in
the Grayville Cemetery

the old settlers of Edwards County, who now survive and shared her hospitality call her memory blessed.[29]

Mainstay of her family, pioneer, nurse, hostess, innkeeper, and heroine of an unusual love story, Eliza Julia was no ordinary woman.

Epilogue

In 1850, just four years after George had inherited it from his mother, Park House was sold to Thomas Mumford of Indiana at a terrible financial sacrifice. This beautiful house in its parklike setting that had meant so much to so many settlers and visitors was a house designed for expensive and gracious living. Since there were not many well-to-do families interested in it, Park House changed hands several times more in the next dozen years before being totally destroyed by fire in the mid-1860s, a sad end for a house that had once been known as the finest house west of the Allegheny Mountains. On the other hand, perhaps it might actually have been a better way for an elegant country house to go than through abandonment with accompanying slow deterioration and degradation.

When a county road running north of Park House was widened after World War I, the family graveyard was moved. Few remains were found other than the family stone, that of patriarch Richard Flower, which was moved to the cemetery in Albion. The only indication of the site of Park House now existing is a monument dedicated in the 1940s.

In the summer of 1988, an archaeological dig done by the students of Frontier College unearthed only scattered pottery shards and a few bricks. One hundred twenty-five years of regular plowing and disking had obliterated all traces of the most famous house on the English Prairie.

Eliza Julia's children weathered the years more successfully than the house in which they grew up. Despite the rocky financial start of her marriage with Hugh Pentacost, Eliza Julia's oldest daughter, Emma, managed a successful life. She had six children, among them a son who became a famous evangelist serving at the Bethany Presbyterian Church in Philadelphia and other prominent churches in New York, Boston, and Europe. Emma's descendants include many ministers, in addition to doctors, lawyers, architects, engineers, editors, businessmen, a rather unusual number of musicians and actors, and several authors of national stature.

A monument dedicated in 1942 at the site where Park House had been built

Eliza Julia's minister son, Alfred, also had six children, five of them sons. One was a prominent doctor in Boston, one an editor, also in Boston, and two were ministers. Another son educated as a physician was also a businessman: a charming, flamboyant conman who kept his family in the Waldorf Astoria Hotel in New York City and made his living by luring wealthy easterners to Mexico to invest in gold mines that he had heavily "salted."

Eliza Julia's second daughter, Rosamond, also had six children, one of whom was named Eliza Julia after her mother. Rosamond's home in Grayville became a refuge for her parents in their later years. Like Emma's family, Rosamond's descendants included dancers, poets, and writers.

Camillus Flower, Eliza Julia's second son, farmed the Flower property on the prairie deeded to him by the others. Camillus had twelve children. Of the nine of his twelve children who lived to adulthood, seven, both boys and girls, went west to Washington State, where a western branch of the family was established. In his later years, Camillus and his wife joined their children in the west, leaving the prairie farming to the remaining two sons, Phillip on the English Prairie and Fred on French Creek Prairie. When Phillip's only son later joined his uncles in the west, the last Flower on the English Prairie was gone.

William, who before Eliza Julia's death had caused his mother so much concern by not writing, did in fact later marry and settle down just as his mother had longed for him to do—but not before having a fling in the California gold rush. For a time he was a minority investor in the Comstock mines, but unfortunately he sold his shares before that strike developed into a great success. He became a blacksmith in a little town near Sacramento, where he met and married a widow. They had one son. When William died in an accident riding horseback, he left behind him a well-established reputation for "kindness and gentleness." Eliza Julia would have been pleased that the "kind, gentle boy" remained so.

Richard, killed in the Civil War, left one son, Henry, who was brought up in Kansas by his mother after she remarried. Henry became a successful lawyer, banker, and railroad president. If Eliza Julia could have known that Henry's three children were all well educated at some of the best schools in the country, it would certainly have satisfied her ardent desire for education for her children and perhaps eased any disappointment she might have harbored because of her son Richard's lack of scholarship and opportunity for education.

Mary, the youngest daughter, was Eliza Julia's good right arm and stayed close to her mother. She postponed marriage until she was nearly thirty and continued to help Eliza Julia until her mother's death. Mary was with her parents when they died in Grayville. She died shortly after her parents at the age of thirty-six, leaving two small sons who were brought up by the McArthurs, her husband's family.

Benjamin, Eliza Julia's youngest child, died in his mid-twenties leaving no issue.[1]

Albion, described by Eliza Julia in her first letter to John as "the town which Mr. Flower and his father and some other gentlemen founded some years since" exists today as a pleasant, busy twentieth-century community, with a town square and a brick courthouse.

The Flowers were instrumental in establishing Albion as the county seat of Edwards County as early as 1821. This distinction was a good foundation for its growth. It was the market town for a large area of the county and grew to be a prosperous small southeastern Illinois town. The residents weathered the vagaries of business cycles accented by inflationary periods and bank failures, as Albion reflected state and national economic and political trends.

Albion and Edwards County never became the wool center the Flowers had hoped that it would be. Hogs became as important to the economy as wool had been envisioned to be. The immense number of hogs raised led to the establishment in the mid-nineteenth century of several packing houses, the largest of which, owned by C. S. Stewart, packed three thousand hogs a season, shipping principally to Cincinnati and points east. There is a Stewart's store on the Albion square today. Albion remains a center for pork production.

Flour mills were important to the prosperity of Albion, but more unusual were the wagon and plow factories. The heavy prairie sod required and led to the invention by the

Painter and Frankland Plow Works of the famous "stump plow" especially designed to break through heavy prairie grass. Painter and Frankland's factory commenced operations in 1868 and produced seventy wagons and six hundred plows a year. It is possible today to buy hard-to-find tools at the Painter and Frankland hardware store on the square.

The economic focus of Edwards County through the years remained principally agricultural, and since 1857 the annual fair is the highlight of the summer, another inheritance from those early days when the Flowers and others organized the first agricultural fair in the state of Illinois in 1825.

The English Settlement left other marks on those who inherited Albion. The kiln that Richard Flower built was the first in the county, and the bricks it produced from the excellent clay of the county led to much more brick-making. For many years one of Albion's most prosperous manufactories was the Bassett and Son's brickyard, begun in 1850 and continued well into the twentieth century. A strong brick suitable for paving was the basis for beautiful well-paved brick streets, many of which are still in use. Brick was also used for building substantial homes, churches, and hotels. After the middle of the nineteenth century, the most successful of the immigrants built large brick homes both in and around the town, and many of these buildings reflect an English style of architecture first introduced in the Flowers' Park House. Albion continued to reflect the cultured life exemplified by the founders.

Things did not change quickly in Edwards County. Many of the residents today bear the same surnames as those of the earliest settlers, names that appear on the manifest of the first shipload of immigrants recruited by George Flower in 1817.

Eliza Julia's letters, which are central to this book, are part of the literature of the Illinois-Indiana frontier. Books written in the first decades of the nineteenth century by the many travelers who came to visit the region attracted additional visitors and many settlers. Letters written by the early settlers to their families and friends in England are particularly interesting because they describe in the most basic terms the lives that the settlers led, their trials, and their aspirations.

The special significance of Eliza Julia's letters is that from them one obtains a richly detailed picture of life in southeastern Illinois at a time, the 1830s–50s, when not much attention was paid to the region that from 1817 to 1825 had enjoyed the center of the stage. After 1825 the growth of Chicago and the development of northern Illinois drew public attention in that direction, and not much was written about Albion, Edwards County, or southeastern Illinois after that time.

Eliza Julia's letters make it clear that the Flowers worked as hard as any other settlers, American or English, but reveal that they were different from their neighbors in important ways. At the outset they had more money than most of the others. They were well educated and interested in music and other cultural activities. They built libraries and schools as well as brick kilns and cotton gins. They were from the upper middle class of English society.

An additional assessment of Eliza Julia can be made by comparing her life with that of Rebecca Burlend, an English countrywoman from Yorkshire, who settled in Pike County in western Illinois in 1831.[2] Mrs. Burlend had been a farm worker in England and found hard work in America no great surprise. In her book, which she dictated to her schoolteacher son in England, Mrs. Burlend described her life in Illinois with her husband and three young children as a constant battle for survival against poverty, weather, and adversity. At the end of their second year, however, by virtue of hard work, luck, and good neighbors, the Burlends began to build a successful life on the western Illinois frontier. They harvested some surpluses, even rented some of their land to others. The Burlends did not attempt to build a town or ameliorate the lives of slaves or read home and foreign newspapers, as did the Flowers. Eliza Julia was different from Rebecca Burlend in that she had no experience with manual labor before she came to Illinois and so must have found frontier life nearly overwhelming. Yet these two women were alike in that they worked hard from morning to night, and their families could not have succeeded as well as they did if they had not had many children with whom to share the labor. Similar, yet dissimilar, both of them lived full and interesting lives and contributed, each in her own way, to the development of Illinois and the United States of America.

Although the literature of the frontier is full of stories of the toil of women and the backbreaking work of men, it is important to remember that not all of frontier life was drudgery. From reading her letters one might conclude that Eliza Julia was a complainer, since she wrote to John about the daily work that kept her busy from before dawn until after dusk. A careful reading of these letters shows that she was not complaining, but instead trying to prepare her nephews for life on the prairie as it truly was. Rebecca Burlend's little book is not about complaints either; rather it is an attempt to explain to potential emigrants from the farms of England that life in America would be demanding, if not hazardous, long before it became for them economically rewarding.

It is important to note that life in America really was a better life than many of the immigrants had left in England. English working-class people had never had so much good food or such a pleasant life as they enjoyed in Illinois.[3] Both working-class and upper-middle-class families found that in Illinois they were free from a state church, they could own their own land, they had the right to vote, they enjoyed the beauties of the countryside, and they believed that they had significant opportunities for even better futures. Mrs. Burlend's delight in the prairie must have been shared by many others.

Let the reader imagine himself by the side of a rich meadow, or fine grass plain several miles in diameter, decked with myriads of flowers of a most gorgeous and varied description, and he will have before his mind a pretty correct representation of one of these prairies. Nothing can surpass in richness or colour, or beauty of formation many of the flowers which are found in the most liberal profusion on these extensive and untrodden fields.[4]

Eliza Julia, in one of her letters to John, summed up her view of her life in Illinois,

I like the Backwoods as they are called better than any place on Earth—I came into the country from Choice and I am a thorough American in principle and practice—It is a lovely Country.[5]

Appendix A

Descendants of Richard Flower

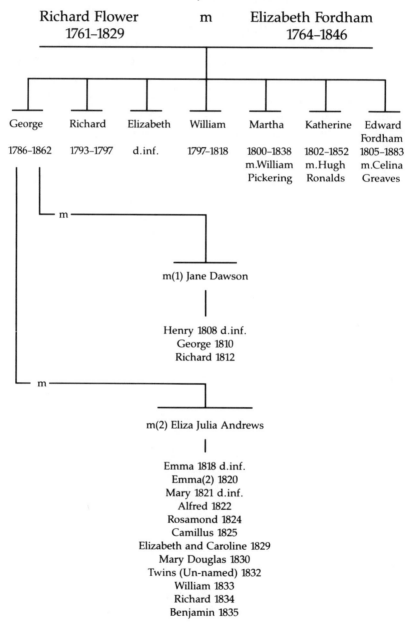

Richard Flower   m   Elizabeth Fordham
1761–1829   1764–1846

George	Richard	Elizabeth	William	Martha	Katherine	Edward Fordham
1786–1862	1793–1797	d.inf.	1797–1818	1800–1838 m.William Pickering	1802–1852 m.Hugh Ronalds	1805–1883 m.Celina Greaves

m

m(1) Jane Dawson

Henry 1808 d.inf.
George 1810
Richard 1812

m

m(2) Eliza Julia Andrews

Emma 1818 d.inf.
Emma(2) 1820
Mary 1821 d.inf.
Alfred 1822
Rosamond 1824
Camillus 1825
Elizabeth and Caroline 1829
Mary Douglas 1830
Twins (Un-named) 1832
William 1833
Richard 1834
Benjamin 1835

Appendix B

Descendants of Mordecai Andrews

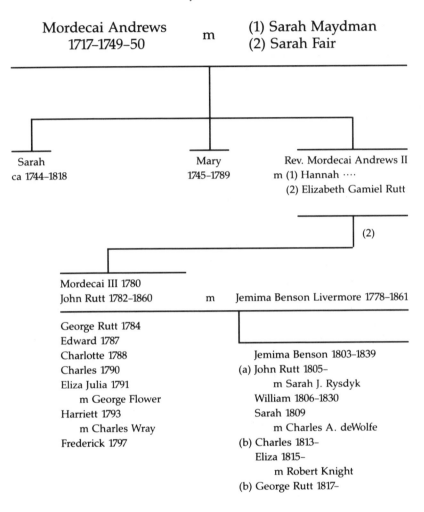

Mordecai Andrews   m   (1) Sarah Maydman
1717–1749–50   (2) Sarah Fair

Sarah
ca 1744–1818

Mary
1745–1789

Rev. Mordecai Andrews II
m (1) Hannah ⋯⋯
(2) Elizabeth Gamiel Rutt

(2)

Mordecai III 1780
John Rutt 1782–1860   m   Jemima Benson Livermore 1778–1861

George Rutt 1784
Edward 1787
Charlotte 1788
Charles 1790
Eliza Julia 1791
   m George Flower
Harriett 1793
   m Charles Wray
Frederick 1797

Jemima Benson 1803–1839
(a) John Rutt 1805–
   m Sarah J. Rysdyk
William 1806–1830
Sarah 1809
   m Charles A. deWolfe
(b) Charles 1813–
Eliza 1815–
   m Robert Knight
(b) George Rutt 1817–

(a) Nephew with whom Eliza Julia corresponded.

(b) Nephew who came to Eliza Julia Flower.

Chart draft courtesy of B. P. Walker

Appendix C

Town of Albion Articles of Agreement [Richard Flower]

This indenture made and entered into this fourteenth day of October in the year of our Lord one thousand and eight hundred and eighteen between Richard Flower, George Flower, Charles Pugsley, Charles Trimmer, Hugh Ronalds and Benjamin Grut of the County of Edwards, State of Illinois and Samuel Thompson of London in Great Britain.

Witnesseth:

That the above parties do hereby agree to form themselves into a company for the purpose of selecting an eligible tract of land and laying out a town thereon. In furtherance of which object the said parties do agree to raise a joint stock to the amount of four thousand dollars, by means of eight equal shares of five hundred dollars each of which the above named Richard Flower does agree to take two shares and the remaining before named six persons one share each to have and to hold the same to them, their heirs, executors, administrators and assigns forever. The amount of the share shall be paid in such instalments as the company may direct and the parties do further agree that the amount of the stock or the number of the shares shall not be increased without the unanimous consent of the whole company. And the said shareholders for the better management of their interest in the said town do hereby for themselves, their heirs, executors and administrators, covenant and agree as follows, to wit:

1stly   The shares aforesaid may be transferred, sold, alienated and conveyed by their respective owners at pleasure, provided, however that in each and every transfer or conveyance whereby any share in the said town shall be a stipulation to the effect following, to wit: That the purchaser or purchasers shall in all things be governed by the covenants, stipulations and agreements in this article of agreement until the same shall expire by its own limitations.

2ndly   A majority of the shareholders shall have the right to establish and prescribe such rules and regulations in all things relating to the concerns of said town as to them shall appear most needful and beneficial and may designate and lay off the town in such form and in lots of such size as to them shall seem best, and may reserve for the public use so much thereof as will be necessary for public square buildings, colleges, academic school houses and houses of public worship and may sell and convey the lots of the said town in such numbers and upon such terms as to them shall seem best and when any lot shall be sold or any agreement shall be made by a majority of the shareholders concerning said town each and every shareholder when therewith required by such majority shall sign, seal and deliver the necessary deeds, conveyances, vouchers and papers.

3rdly   Where any act concerning the said town or any lot thereof shall be done and performed by or under the direction of the majority of the shareholders the same shall be binding and obligatory upon each and every shareholder, and this article of agreement shall be an effectual bar against any relief to be sought in law or equity by any shareholder or shareholders against such act so done and performed.

4thly   Upon any question touching the objects of this article of agreement the shareholders shall be entitled to one vote each and no more.

5thly   The shareholders aforesaid or their executors, administrators or assigns of such a measure shall be determined upon by a majority of the shareholders may annex to the said town other lands than those necessary for the scite [sic] of the town aforesaid, which lands when so annexed shall in all things be subject to the regulations, covenants, and agreements contained in this indenture.

6thly   This article of agreement shall continue in force for the term of four years commencing from the first day of January in the year of our Lord one thousand eight hundred and nineteen fully to be completed and ended.

7thly   On the first day of January one thousand eight hundred and twenty three the expiration of the term of time aforesaid the property of the town aforesaid together with such as may be added thereto by virtue of this agreement—if any shall be so added—shall be divided and partition thereof be made among the several shareholders according to the number of shares owned by them respectively, or the same property shall be sold and parted among the shareholders as a majority may determine. Should a majority of the shareholders however wish to continue a joint concern in the town aforesaid either under this article of agreement or any other after the expiration of the term of time aforesaid a fair and full evaluation of the property shall be made in such manner as shall be agreed upon by the shareholders and such as declare to continue as aforesaid their joint interest shall be paid in money the value of their respective shares made as above provided.

8thly   It is necessary to observe that altho' for various reasons the signatures have been withheld from this article of agreement since the 14th day of October 1818 to this second day of August 1819, the aformentioned shareholders do nevertheless acknowledge particularly all the actions, bye-laws and resolutions passed or made since the fourteenth day of October, 1818 aforesaid to this day and approve and confirm the same as their free and unanimous acts for the benefit of the joint stock company aforesaid.*

9thly   And whereas, Samuel Thompson, now of the city of London in Great Britain has his interest in this company represented by George Flower, the remaining members of the said joint stock company do hereby recognize his signature for the said Samuel Thompson as valid and of full effect as if the latter were present personally to subscribe his own signature hereto.

10thly   For the full and faithful performance of each and every article, stipulation and agreement herein contained the said Richard Flower, George Flower, Charles Pugsley, Charles Trimmer, Hugh Ronalds, and Benjamin Grut do hereby each for himself (and George Flower on behalf of Samuel Thompson) his heirs, executors and administrators bind himself to the other, his heirs, executors, administrators and assigns, in the penal sum of two thousand dollars.

In testimony whereof they have herewith set their hands and seals this second day of August aforesaid, in the year of our Lord one thousand eight hundred and nineteen.

---

*Richard Flower did not arrive in Albion until the summer of 1819.

Signed and Sealed in the presence of	(Seal)	Richard Flower
	(Seal)	George Flower
Henry Bowman	(Seal)	Chas. Pugsley
Jno Craddock	(Seal)	Chas. Trimmer
	(Seal)	Hugh Ronalds
	(Seal)	Benjamin Grut
	(Seal)	George Flower, atty. for Samuel Thompson

NOTES

Introduction

1. George Flower, *History of the English Settlement in Edwards County, Illinois,* edited by E. B. Washburne. Chicago, Chicago Historical Society Collections, 1882, p. 27

2. Elias Pym Fordham, *Personal Narrative of Travels in Virginia, Maryland, Pennsylvania, Ohio, Indiana, and Kentucky: And of a Residence in the Illinois Territory: 1817–1818,* edited by Frederic Austin Ogg, Cleveland, Ohio, Arthur H. Clark Company, 1906, p. 21

3. G. Flower to Judge Peters, letter in the Historical Society of Pennsylvania, photocopy in Knox College Library, Galesburg, Illinois

4. Morris Birkbeck, *Notes on a Journey in America,* London for James Ridgway, 1818, and *Letters from Illinois,* London, Taylor and Hessey, 1818, reprinted, New York, Augustus M. Kelley, 1971, pp. 32, 33

5. Flower, *History,* p. 49

6. Ibid., p. 64

7. B. P. Birch, *The Environment and Settlement of the Prairie–Woodland Transition Belt—A Case Study of Edwards County, Illinois,* Southampton Research Series in Geography, Number Six, June 1971, edited by R. J. Small, Southampton, Department of Geography, Southampton University, p. 10

8. Allen Nevins, "Not Without Thy Wondrous Story, Illinois," *An Illinois Reader,* edited by Clyde C. Walton. Dekalb, Northern Illinois Press, 1970, p. 7

9. William Faux, *Memorable Days in America,* in R. G. Thwaites, *Early Western Travels,* Cleveland, Ohio, Arthur H. Clark Company, 1905, pp. 276, 277

10. Birkbeck, *Notes,* pp. 32, 33

11. Jane Louise Mesick, *The English Traveler in America,* Ithaca, Cornell University Press, 1922, republished 1970; also Jane Rodman, "The English Settlement in Southern Illinois as Viewed by English Travelers, 1815–1825," *Indiana Magazine of History,* XLIV, March 1948, pp. 37–68. A very full and helpful review of this literature.

12. Solon J. Buck, *Travel and Description, 1765–1865,* Springfield, Illinois State Historical Society Library, 1914, Biographical Series, Vol. II, p. 13

13. Flower, *History,* p. 93

14. Paul Angle, "Morris Birkbeck: Illustrious Illinoisan," *Chicago History,* Vol. VIII, No. 5, Fall 1967, p. 144, and Charles Boewe, *Prairie Albion,* Carbondale, Southern Illinois University Press, 1962.

15. Theodore Calvin Pease, *The Story of Illinois,* Chicago, University of Chicago Press, 3rd revision, Marguerite Jenison Pease, 1965, p. 89

16. Mary Ann Salter, "Quarreling in the English Settlement: the Flowers in Court," *Journal of the Illinois Historical Society,* LXXV/2/Summer, 1982, p. 101–14. Also Keith Linus Miller, *Building Towns on the Southeastern*

Illinois Frontier 1810–1830, doctoral dissertation, Miami University, Oxford, Ohio, 1976

17. *Diary of William Owen,* edited by Joel W. Hiatt, 1906, Indianapolis, Bobbs Merrill, reprinted by Augustus M. Kelley, Clifton, N. J., 1973 by arrangement with the Indiana Historical Society, p. 103

18. Walter Colyer, "Walter Mayo, A Pioneer of Edwards County," *Journal of the Illinois Historical Society,* Vol, 5, April 1912, pp. 83–84

19. *Diaries of Donald McDonald,* 12824–26, Indiana Historical Society Publications, Vol. 14, Number 2, Indianapolis, 1942, p. 258, and, *Diary of William Owen,* p. 93

20. John A. Jakle, *Images of the Ohio Valley, A Historical Geography of Travel, 1740–1860,* N. Y., Oxford Press, 1977, pp. 170–173

21. Roy A. Billington, "The Frontier in Illinois History," *Journal of the Illinois Historical Society,* Vol. XLIII, 1950, p. 32

22. *An Illinois Reader,* edited by Clyde C. Walton, Dekalb, Illinois, Northern Illinois University Press, 1970, p. 35

23. Flower, *History,* p. 123

24. Faux, *Memorable Days in America,* p. 254

25. Robert Dale Owen, letter to Sarah Bolton, 6 July 1851, New Harmony Collection, Indiana State Historical Society, Indianapolis, Indiana

26. Flower, *History,* p. 122fn.

Chapter 1

1. Richard Flower to son Edward, 1 December 1825, Flower Family Papers, Chicago Historical Society Manuscripts

2. Richard Flower to son Edward, 12 December 1825, "George has just returned," Flower Family Papers, Chicago Historical Society Manuscripts

3. Hugh Ronalds to Edward Flower, 15 February 1826, Flower Family Papers, Chicago Historical Society Manuscripts. "Flim's" Ferry, although it has this spelling in family letters and has been seen in print this way, was probably Flynn's—a notorious ferry twenty miles below Shawneetown, run by a troublemaker named Flynn, who before starting his own ferry was a member of the infamous Ford Gang near Cave-in-Rock.

4. Martha Pickering (Mrs. William Pickering) to Edward Flower, 20 August 1825, Flower Family Papers, Chicago Historical Society Manuscripts

5. Celia Morris Eckhardt, *Fanny Wright, Rebel in America,* Cambridge, Massachusetts, Harvard University Press, 1984, p. 148

6. *Robert Dale Owen's Travel Journal, 1827,* edited by Josephine M. Elliott, Indianapolis, Indiana Historical Society, 1977, p. 40

7. A. J. C. Perkins and Theresa Wolfson, *Frances Wright Free Enquirer: The Study of a Temperament,* New York and London, Harper and Brothers, 1939, p. 135

8. Perkins and Wolfson, p. 136

9. Eckhardt, p. 108

10. Faux, *Memorable Days In America,* p. 275

11. P. L. Illinois, 9 ga 2 session, p. 259–60

12. Eckhardt, p. 122

13. Madame Charles de Lasteyrie, wife of the brother-in-law of LaFayette, was the only woman of that family to remain loyal to Fanny Wright.

14. The Garnetts were friends of the Wrights who lived with them in their New Jersey home from 1819 to 1820 and maintained a warm correspondence thereafter.

15. Perkins and Wolfson, p. 135

16. Cecilia Helena Payne-Gaposchkin, *The Nashoba Plan for Removing the Evil of Slavery: Letters of Frances and Camilla Wright, 1820–1829,* Harvard Library Bulletin, Vol. 23, No. 3, July 1975, p. 432

17. Payne-Gaposchkin, p. 433

18. Camilla Wright to Julia and Harriet Garnett, Payne-Gaposchkin, p. 439

19. Ibid, p. 441

20. Eckhardt, p. 132

21. Frances Trollope, *Domestic Manners of the Americans,* Barre, Massachusetts: The Imprint Society, 1969, p. 25

22. Interview with William Fordham Flower, great-great-grandson of George and Eliza Julia Flower

Chapter 2

1. Faux, *Memorable Days in America,* p. 254

2. Ibid, p. 254

3. James Madison, *The Indiana Way, A State History,* Indianapolis, Indiana Historical Society, Bloomington: Indiana University Press, 1986, pp. 63ff

4. Agnes Rothery, *Family Album,* New York: Dodd, Mead and Company, 1942, p. 67

5. John Woods, *Two Years' Residence in the Settlement on the English Prairie,* London, 1822, pp. 214–15

6. Flower, *History,* p. 69

7. Alice Felt Tyler, *Freedom's Ferment,* New York: Harper and Row, 1962, p. 22

8. Edwards County (Illinois) Courthouse, Office of Circuit County Clerk, Box #8, *The People vs. Jas. Kennedy et al.,* filed July 8, 1825

9. George Flower to his sister, 4 September 1816, Illinois State Historical Library Manuscripts, Flower Box 1

10. Richard Flower, *Letters from Lexington and the Illinois,* London, C. Teulon For Ridgway, 1819, p. 26

11. James Stuart, *Three Years in North America,* Edinburgh, 1833, p. 386

12. Richard Flower, *Letters,* p. 23–24

13. Fred Gustorf, "Frontier Perils Told by an Early Illinois Visitor," *Journal of the Illinois Historical Society,* Vol. 55, 1962, pp. 142–43

14. Letter from William Dobell to Mrs. Lucy Coveney, January 6, 1842, *Journal of the Illinois Historical Society*, Vol 15, Nos. 1–2, 1922–23, p. 527

15. George Flower, *Errors of Immigrants*, reprint of 1841 edition, New York: Arno Press, 1975, p. 26

Chapter 3

1. Eliza Julia learned from her nephew John that his brother William, about whom she had inquired in her last letter, had died in Calcutta, India, about 1830. He would have been twenty-four years old: Andrews Family Records, Dorothy Robinson, Watertown, N. Y.

2. Flower, *History*, p. 107

3. *Diary of William Owen*, pp. 63, 67–68

4. Grant Foreman, "English Settlers in Illinois," *Journal of the Illinois State Historical Society*, Vol 34, No. 3, Sept., 1941, pp. 315, 317–18

5. George Flower, *Errors of Immigrants*, p. 9

6. Flower, *History*, p. 299

7. Charles Dickens, *American Notes for General Circulation*, London, 1842, reprinted in Paul Angle, *Prairie State, Impressions of Illinois, 1673–1967, by Travelers and Other Observers*, Chicago and London: University of Chicago Press, 1968, p. 207

8. Otto A. Rothert, *The Outlaws of Cave-in-Rock*, Cleveland: Arthur C. Clark, 1924

9. Content of this letter indicates it was written 16 July although dated 16 June 1833

10. Robert P. Sutton, editor, *The Prairie State, Colonial Years to 1860*, Grand Rapids, Michigan, W. B. Eerdmans Publishing Company, 1976, p. 155

11. John Woods, *Two Years' Residence in the Settlement on the English Prairie*, London, 1822, p. 128–130

12. Pease, *The Frontier State*, p. 8

13. Ibid, p. 9

14. James Hall, *Letters from the West; Containing Sketches of Scenery, Manners, and Customs; and Anecdotes Connected with the First Settlement of the Western Section of the United States*, London, 1828, pp. 88ff

Chapter 4

1. Ray A. Billington, "The Frontier in Illinois History," *Journal of the Illinois Historical Society*, Vol. 43, No. 1, Spring 1950, p. 31

2. Donald Tingley, "Anti-Intellectualism on the Illinois Frontier," *Essays in Illinois History*, edited by Donald F. Tingley, Carbondale, Illinois, Southern Illinois University Press, 1968, p. 7

3. Interview with Janet Flower, Portland, Oregon (Eliza Julia's great-great-granddaughter)

4. This letter of September 1, 1833, is a copy: the only letter in the Robinson collection that is not original, made when the original was sent to Dr. G. F. Pentacost, Eliza Julia's grandson, 8 August 1895.

5. Solon J. Buck, *Illinois 1818*, 2nd Edition, Chicago, Illinois Centennial Committee, 1917, pp. 165–66

6. Pease, *Story of Illinois*, p. 97

7. *Diary of William Owen*, p. 81

8. Flower, *History*, Letter to George Flower, May 12, 1825, from Donald MacDonald, p. 374

9. Edgar L. Dukes, *Yesteryears in Edwards County, Illinois*, Albion, Illinois, printed by the author (two volumes, Vol. 1, 1945, Vol 2, 1948), Vol 2, p. 81

10. Flower, *History*, p. 338–39

11. Dukes, vol. II, p. 82

12. Ibid, p. 82

13. The partnership between Robert Owen and William McClure gave the latter sole charge of the educational effort in New Harmony. McClure had visited Pestalozzi's school in Switzerland and was convinced of the usefulness of the system. He had established a school in Pennsylvania from which he brought teachers to New Harmony. In 1826, he outlined the system of instruction to organize a boarding school in New Harmony that would teach mechanism, mathematics, science, writing, drawing, music, languages, gymnastics, and manual training. The schools established primarily for the children of the community were open on payment of tuition to children from outside. The terms for non-residents were $100 per annum: George Lockwood, *The New Harmony Movement*, New York, D. C. Appleton & Company, 1905, p. 239

14. *Life and Writing of George Edward Flower*, edited by Isaac Errett, Cincinnati, Standard Publishing Company, 1885, p. 14. George Edward Flower was a grandson of Eliza Julia's, the son of her eldest son, Alfred. The books mentioned in the grandson's biography in 1885 are the same books, the library of Richard Flower, mentioned in Eliza Julia's letter of August 8, 1834.

15. Flower, R., *Letters from the Illinois*, p. 17

16. William Dobell, "Original Letters—A Description of the Illinois Country," Letter to Mrs. Lucy Coveney, *Journal of the Illinois Historical Society*, Vol. 15, April 1922 to January 1923, pp. 529–30

17. Robert Gehlman Bone, "Education in Illinois Before 1857," *Journal of the Illinois Historical Society*, Vol. 50, No. 2, Summer, 1957, p. 128

18. *Parley's Magazine* was written and published by Samuel Griswold Goodrich, whose first book, *Tales of Peter Parley about America*, was published in Boston in 1827. He wrote many more books for young people and published *Parley's Magazine* in 1833 and 1834.

19. Katherine and Hugh Ronalds left on 11 October 1832 for an extended visit to England. Taking their two eldest children, Kate and Hugh, with them, they left two small daughters at Park House with their grandmother, Elizabeth Flower. It was these girls, Jane and Emily, to whom Eliza Julia was referring. The baby, Francis, was left in the care of Mrs.

Shepherd, the Flowers' long-time nanny. Kate Ronalds gave birth to her sixth child, Richard Braddock, at Braddock Fields, Pennsylvania, on 10 January 1833. Her health was so fragile that they had stopped there for the winter, continuing on to England in the spring. Kate's poor health kept them in England with Ronalds and Flower relatives until the spring of 1835.

Chapter 5

1. *The Life and Writings of George E. Flower*, p. 24

2. Richard Flower, *Letters from the Illinois*, p. 19

3. Adlard Welby, *A Visit to North America and the English Settlements in Illinois*, London: J. Drury, 1821, reprinted, editor, Reuben Gold Thwaites, *Early Western Travels, 1748–1846*, Cleveland, Ohio, 1905, p. 252

4. Flower, G., *History*, p. 132

5. George Flower, *Errors of Emigrants*, London: Cleave, 1841, reprinted, New York: Arno, 1975, p. 35

6. Mary Katherine Ronalds to Edward Flower, 12 July 1827, Chicago Historical Society Manuscript Division, Chicago, Illinois, Flower Family Papers

7. *History of Edwards County, Illinois*, Vol. I, Edwards County Historical Society, Albion, Illinois: Taylor Publishing Company, Dallas, Texas, 1980, p. 144

8. Edgar Dukes, *Yesteryears in Edwards County*, Vol. 1, p. 111

9. Interview, Janet Flower, Portland, Oregon

10. Morris Birkbeck, *Letters from Illinois*, p. 68

11. Richard J. Jensen, *Illinois, A Bicentennial History*, New York: W. W. Norton and Company, 1978, pp. 12–13

12. Robert P. Howard, *Illinois, A History of the Prairie State*, Grand Rapids, Michigan: William B. Eerdmans Publishing Company, 1972, pp. 113–14

13. Keith L. Miller, "Planning, Proper Hygiene, and a Doctor. The Good Health of the English Settlement," *Journal of the Illinois Historical Society*, February 1978, p. 26

14. William N. Blane, *An Excursion Through the United States and Canada During the Years 1822–23 by an English Gentleman*, London, 1824

15. Fred Gustorf, "Frontier Perils Told by an Early Illinois Visitor," *Journal of the Illinois Historical Society*, Vol. 55, 1962, p. 145

16. George Flower to his brother Edward, 23 January 1826, Flower Family Papers, Chicago Historical Society

Chapter 6

1. Flower, *History*, p. 328

2. Ibid, pp. 132–33

3. Mary Katherine Ronalds to her brother Edward, 25 February 1839, Chicago Historical Society, Chicago, Illinois, Flower Family Papers

4. James Stuart, *Three Years in America*, vol. 2, p. 383

5. Dukes, *Yesteryears,* Vol. 1, p. 34

6. Betty Madden, *Arts and Crafts and Architecture in Early Illinois,* Urbana, Illinois State Museum and the University of Illinois Press, 1974, p. 70

7. Stuart, Vol. 2, p. 384

8 Lewis E. Atherton, *The Frontier Merchant in Mid-America,* Columbia, Missouri: University Press, 1971, pp. 25ff

9. Michael Hartley to an Uncle, August 14, 1829, Edwards County Historical Society, Albion, Illinois

10. Interview, William Fordham Flower, great-great-grandson of Eliza Julia, as told to him by his great aunt, Martha Pickering Flower

11. Thomas Ford, *A History of Illinois, From Its Commencement as a State in 1818 to 1847,* Chicago: S. C. Griggs, 1854, pp. 96–97

12. *History of Gallatin, Saline, Hamilton, Franklin and Williamson Counties,* published by Goodspeed, 1887, pp. 92, 98, 101

13. Karl Arndt, *A Documentary History of the Indiana Decade of the Harmony Society, 1814–1824,* Indiana Historical Society, Indianapolis: Vol. 2, pp. 579–80

14. Ibid, pp. 734, 806, 814

15. Warder Bros. to Edward F. Flower, November 19, 1827, Chicago Historical Society Manuscripts, Flower Family Papers

16. George Edward Flower, *Life and Writings,* p. 13

17. G. Flower, *History,* p. 158

18. Howard, p. 171

19. Josephine Boylan, "Illinois Highways, 1700–1848, Roads, Rivers, Ferries, Canals," *Journal of the Illinois Historical Society,* Vol. 26, No. 1–2, April–July, 1933, p. 25

20. Ford, pp. 182ff

21. Eliza Julia Flower to N. F. Nettleton, 29 June 1844, Illinois State Historical Library, Flower Papers, Box 1

22. Eliza Julia to Nettleton, July 25, 1844, Illinois State Historical Library, Flower Papers, Box 1

23. Ibid, Nettleton letter, July 25, 1844, p. 2

24. Ford, *A History of Illinois,* p. 44

25. Ibid, p. 47

26. Edgar L Dukes, "George Flower of Albion Seeks a Loan," *Journal of the Illinois Historical Society,* Vol. 49, No. 2, Summer 1956, pp. 221–27

27. Miller, *Building Towns,* p. 29

Chapter 7

1. Posey County (Indiana) Record Book, Vol. 5, No. 167, p. 175, Barbara (Ramsey) Smith, Compiler

2. George Flower to William Barry, July 19, 1860, Illinois State Historical Library, Flower Papers, Box 1

3. G. Flower to unidentified lawyer, February 1860, Illinois State Historical Library, Flower Papers

4. Robert Dale Owen (son of Robert Owen) to Sarah Bolton, July 6, 1851, New Harmony Collection, Indiana Historical Society Library, Indianapolis

5. Clipping, believed to be from the New Harmony *Times*, Private Collection of Josephine Elliott, New Harmony, Indiana

6. Mt. Vernon (Indiana) *Advocate*, March 30, 1855, New Harmony Collection, Workingmen's Institute, New Harmony, Indiana

7. Posey County Record Book, Vol. 5, No. 167, p. 175

8. Posey County, Mt. Vernon, Microfilm—Workingmen's Institute, New Harmony, Indiana

9. *Great Aunt Sarah's Diary*, 1846–92, privately printed, 1964, Millbrook Press, Southampton, Warwickshire, England, 25

10. Eliza Julia Flower to her son Camillus, April 4, 1858, original, Patricia Flower Martin, Medical Lake, Washington

11. Mary McArthur to her brother Camillus, January 13, 1858, Martin Collection

12. Deed Record Book, Posey County, Mt. Vernon, Indiana, Book W, 1858

13. Posey County, Mt. Vernon, Microfilm, Workingmen's Institute, New Harmony, Indiana

14. Mary Flower McArthur to her sister-in-law, Edith Prichard Flower, February 24, 1859, Martin Collection

15. G. Flower, *History*, p. 354

16. Manuscript, Chicago Historical Society, Flower Papers

17. Eliza Julia Flower to Camillus and Edith Flower, Mt. Vernon, Indiana, March 1, 1859, Martin Collection

18. Mary McArthur to Camillus Flower, February 17, 1859, Martin Collection

19. Mary McArthur to Camillus Flower, February 27, 1859, Martin Collection

20. Benjamin Flower to Camillus Flower, January 28, 1858, Martin Collection

21. Mary McArthur to Camillus Flower, January 13, 1858, Martin Collection

22. Eliza Julia to Camillus Flower, February 28, 1859, Martin Collection

23. Richard Flower to Camillus Flower, October 24, 1861, Martin Collection

24. Richard Flower to Camillus Flower, October 24, 1861, Martin Collection

25. Flower family genealogy, compiled 1966 by Henry C. Flower, Jr., Greenwich, Connecticut, great-grandson of George Flower, assisted by Janet Flower, Portland, Oregon. Copy supplied by Janet Flower.

26. *Great Aunt Sarah's Diary*, p. 49

27 George Flower, *History*, Preface, Chicago Historical Society, 1882, p. 12

28. *History of Edwards, Lawrence and Wabash Counties*, Illinois: J. L. McDonough & Co., Philadelphia, 1883, p. 214-A

29. Ibid, p. 213

Epilogue

1. All information about Eliza Julia's descendants found in the epilogue comes from the Flower family genealogy, Henry C. Flower, 1966

2. Rebecca Burlend, *A True Picture of Emigration*, ed. Milo Milton Quaife, Chicago: The Lakeside Press, R. R. Donnelly and Sons, 1936

3. Grant Foreman, "English Settlers in Illinois," *Journal of the Illinois Historical Society*, Vol. 34, No. 3, Spring 1941

4. Burlend, p. 84

5. Eliza Julia Flower to John Rutt Andrews, 11 March 1833

Selected Bibliography

Angle, Paul. "Morris Birkbeck: Illustrious Illinoisan." *Chicago History* VIII.5 (Fall 1967).

———. *The Prairie State*. Compiled and edited by Paul Angle. Chicago and London: University of Chicago Press, 1968.

Andrews, John Rutt. *Andrews Family Records*.

Arndt, K. J. R. *Documentary History of the Indiana Decade of the Harmony Society, 1814–1824*. Indianapolis: Indiana Historical Society, 1978.

Atherton, Lewis E. *The Frontier Merchant in Mid-America*. Columbia: University of Missouri Press, 1971.

Bestor, Arthur Eugene, Jr. *Backwoods Utopia*. Philadelphia: University of Pennsylvania Press, 1950.

Billington, Roy A. "The Frontier in Illinois History." *Journal of the Illinois State Historical Society*, 43 (Spring 1950).

Birch, B. P. *The Environment and Settlement of the Prairie-Woodland Transition Belt—A Case Study of Edwards County, Illinois*. Edited by R. J. Small. Southhampton Research Series in Geography, Number Six. Southhampton: Department of Geography, Southhampton University, June 1971.

Birkbeck, Morris. *Notes on a Journey in America, from the Coast of Virginia to the Territory of Illinois*. 3d ed. London: James Ridgway, 1818.

———. *Letters from Illinois*. London: Taylor and Hessey, 1818, reprinted, New York: Augustus M. Kelley, 1971.

Birkbeck, Robert. "Morris Birkbeck: Eminent Englishman." *Indiana Magazine of History* 31 (1935).

Blane, William N. *An Excursion through the United States and Canada During the Years 1822–23 by an English Gentleman*. London: Baldwin Cradock & Joy, 1824.

Boewe, Charles. *Prairie Albion*. Carbondale: Southern Illinois University Press, 1962.

Bone, Robert Gehlman. "Education in Illinois before 1837." *Journal of the Illinois State Historical Society* 50. 2 (Summer 1957).

Bonnemains, J. "Lesueur en Amérique du Nord dossier 61." Annales du Muséum du Havre. No. 30. 1986 Place du Vieux-Marché, Le Havre, France 76600.

Boylan, Josephine. "Illinois Highways, 1700–1848, Roads, Rivers, Ferries, Canals." *Journal of the Illinois State Historical Society* 26. 1–2 (April–July, 1933).

Buck, Solon. *Illinois in 1818*. Illinois Centennial Commission, 1917, reprint, University of Illinois Press, I.S.H.S., 1967.

———. *Travel and Description, 1765–1865*. Springfield: Illinois State Historical Society Library, 1914.

Burlend, Rebecca. *A True Picture of Emigration*. Edited by Milo Milton Quaife. Chicago: The Lakeside Press, R. R. Donnelly and Sons, 1936.

Buley, R. Carlyle. *The Old Northwest, Pioneer Period, 1815–1840*. Indianapolis: Indiana Historical Society, 1950.

Circuit Clerk, Edwards County Courthouse, Albion, Illinois, *Meredith found guilty of murdering Richard Flower.*

Cobbett, William. *Journal of a A Year's Residence in the United States of America.* London, 1819, reprinted Centaur Press, 1964, Allen Sutton Publisher, 1983.

Colyer, Walter. "Walter Mayo, A Pioneer of Edwards County." *Journal of the Illinois State Historical Society* 5 (April, 1912).

——. "The Fordhams and LaSerres of the English Settlement in Edwards County." *Transactions of the Illinois State Historical Society, 1911.*

Cummings, Sam'l. *The Western Pilot for 1829, Charts of the Ohio River.* Cincinnati, 1829.

Davis, Rodney O. "Politics and Law in Frontier Illinois." *Illinois, Its History and Legacy.* Compiled and edited by Roger D. Bridges and Rodney O. Davis. St. Louis, Missouri: River City Publishers, 1984.

Degler, Carl. *At Odds: Women and the Family in America from the Revolution to the Present.* New York: Oxford University Press, 1980.

Dickens, Charles. *American Notes for General Circulation.* London, 1842.

Dixon, James Main. "The Flower-Birkbeck Settlement at the Illinois." *American Illustrated Methodist Magazine* 7 (May, 1902).

Dobell, William. "Letter to Mrs. Lucy Coveney, January 6 1842." *Journal of the Illinois State Historical Society* 15 (1922–23).

Dukes, Edgar L. *Yesteryears in Edwards County, Illinois.* Two volumes, Albion, Illinois, limited edition, printed by the author, vol. 1, 1945, vol. 2, 1948

——. "George Flower of Albion Seeks a Loan." *Journal of the Illinois State Historical Society* 49.2 (Summer 1956).

Eckhardt, Celia Morris. *Fanny Wright, Rebel in America.* Cambridge: Harvard University Press, 1984.

Elliott, Josephine M., ed. *Robert Dale Owen's Travel Journal.* Indianapolis: Indiana Historical Society, 1977.

Errett, Isaac, ed. *Life and Writings of George Edward Flower.* Cincinnati: Standard, 1885.

Faux, William. *Memorable Days in America, 1819–1820.* London: Printed for Simpkin and Marshall, 1823, reprinted in *Early Western Travels, 1748–1846.* Vol. 11. Edited by Reuben Gold Thwaites. Cleveland, Ohio: Arthur H. Clark Company, 1905.

Fearon, Henry Bradshaw. *Sketches of America: A Narrative of a Journey of Five Thousand Miles Through the Eastern and Western States of America . . . with Remarks on Mr. Birkbeck's "Notes" and "Letters."* 3d ed. London: Strahan and Spottiswoode, Longman, Hurst, Rees, Orne and Browne, 1819.

Flower, Eliza Julia. Letter to Nettleton, 29 June 1844. Illinois State Historical Society Library, Flower Papers

——. Letter to Nettleton, 25 July 1844.

Flower, George. Letter to Robert Barry. Chicago Historical Society Library, Flower Family Papers.

——. Letter to an unidentified lawyer, February 1860. Illinois State Historical Society Library, Flower Box No. 1.

——— . *Errors of Immigrants.* London: Clear, Shoe Lane, Fleet Street, 1841, reprinted New York: Arno Press, 1975.

——— . *Harmonie.* Manuscript, Chicago Historical Society, Flower Family Papers.

——— . *History of the English Settlement in Edwards County, Illinois.* Edited by B. Washburne. Chicago: Illinois Historical Society Collection, 1882.

——— . Letter to Judge Peters. Historical Society of Pennsylvania. Copy in Knox College Library, Galesburg, Illinois.

——— . Letter to his sister, 4 September 1816. Illinois State Historical Society Library, Flower Box 1.

Flower, Richard. Letter to son Edward, 1 December 1825. Chicago Historical Society, Flower Family Papers

——— . Letter to son Edward, 12 December 1825. Chicago Historical Society, Flower Family Papers.

——— . *Letters from Lexington and the Illinois.* London: C. Teulon for Ridgway, 1819.

——— . "A Brief Account of the Present State of the English Settlement in Illinois." In C. J. Ingersoll, *A Discourse on the Influence of America on the Mind.* American Philosophical Society, 18 October 1823.

Ford, Thomas. *A History of Illinois, from its Commencement as a State in 1818 to 1847.* Chicago: S. C. Griggs, 1854.

Fordham, Elias Pym. *Personal Narrative of Travels in Virginia, Maryland, Pennsylvania, Ohio, Indiana and Kentucky: And of a Residence in the Illinois Territory: 1817–1818.* Edited by Frederic Austin Ogg. Cleveland, Ohio: Arthur H. Clark, 1906.

Foreman, Grant. "English Settlers in Illinois." *Journal of the Illinois State Historical Society* 34.3 (September 1941).

History of Gallatin, Saline, Hamilton, Franklin, and Williamson Counties. Chicago: Goodspeed, 1887, also reprinted Evansville, Indiana: Unigraphics, 1967.

Great Aunt Sarah's Diary. Privately published by Ella Flower, Warwickshire, England, 1964.

Gustorf, Fred. "Frontier Perils Told by an Early Illinois Visitor." *Journal of the Illinois State Historical Society* 55 (1962).

Hall, James. *Letters from the West: Containing Sketches of Scenery, Manners, and Customs; and also Anecdotes Connected with the First Settlement of the Western Section of the United States.* London, 1828.

Hartley, Michael. *Letter to Unknown, August 14, 1829.* Edwards County Historical Society Collection, Albion, Illinois.

Hiatt, Joel W., ed., *Diary of William Owen.* Indianapolis: Bobbs Merrill, 1906, reprinted by arrangement with the Indiana Historical Society, Clifton, New Jersey: Augustus M. Kelley, 1973.

Howard, Robert P. *Illinois, a History of the Prairie State.* Grand Rapids, Michigan: William B. Eerdmans, 1972.

Jakle, John A. *Images of the Ohio Valley, A Historical Geography of Travel, 1740–1860.* New York: Oxford Press, 1977.

Jensen, Richard J. *Illinois—A Bicentennial History.* New York: W. W. Norton, 1978.

Leopold, Richard William. *Robert Dale Owen*. Cambridge: Harvard University Press.

Lockwood, George. *The New Harmony Movement*. New York: D. Appleton, 1905.

Madden, Betty. *Arts and Crafts and Architecture in Early Illinois*. Urbana: Illinois State Museum and the University of Illinois Press, 1974.

Madison, James. *The Indiana Way, A State History*. Indianapolis: Indiana Historical Society, Bloomington: Indiana University Press, 1986.

Mesick, Jane Louise. *The English Traveler in America, 1785–1835*. Ithaca: Cornell University Press, 1922, republished, 1970.

Miller, Keith Linus. *Building Towns on the Southeastern Illinois Frontier, 1810–1830*. Doctoral dissertation. Oxford, Ohio: Miami University, The Graduate School, 1976.

Mt. Vernon *Advocate*. 30 March 1855. New Harmony Collection, Indiana Historical Society.

Nevins, Allen. "—not without thy Wondrous Story, Illinois." *An Illinois Reader*. Edited by Clyde C. Walton. DeKalb: Northern Illinois University Press, 1970.

Oliver, William. *Eight Months in Illinois, 1843*. Newcastle Upon Tyne, William Andrew Mitchell, Ann Arbor University Microfilms, 1966.

Owen, Robert Dale. Letter to Sarah Bolton, 6 July 1851. New Harmony Collection, Indiana State Historical Society.

———. *Threading My Way. Twenty-seven Years of Autobiography*. London: Trubner, 1878. Xerox, University Microforms Library Service, Ann Arbor, Michigan.

Pease, Theodore Calvin. *The Frontier State, 1818–1848*. First ed. Springfield: Illinois Centennial Commission, 1918, republished Urbana and Chicago: University of Illinois Press, 1987.

———. *The Story of Illinois*. 3d revision. Marguerite Jenison Pease, Chicago: University of Chicago Press, 1965.

Perkins, A. J. C., and Theresa Wolfson. *Frances Wright Free Enquirer: The Study of a Temperament*. New York and London: Harper and Brothers, 1939.

Pickering, Mrs. Martha. Letter to Edward Flower, 20 August 1825. Chicago Historical Society, Flower Family Papers.

Posey County Record Book. Barbara (Ramsey) Smith, compiler. Vol. 5, 167.

Posey County Deed Record Book. Posey County 1860 Census. Workingmen's Institute, New Harmony, Indiana.

Rodman, Jane. "The English Settlement in Southern Illinois as Viewed by English Travelers, 1815–1825." *Indiana Magazine of History* 44 (March 1948).

Ronalds, Hugh. Letter to Edward Flower, 15 February 1826. Chicago Historical Society, Flower Family Papers.

Ronalds, Mary Katherine. Letter to Edward Flower, 12 July 1827. Flower Family Papers, Chicago Historical Society.

———. Letter to Edward Flower, 25 February 1839. Flower Family Papers, Chicago Historical Society.

Rothert, Otto A. *The Outlaws of Cave-in Rock.* Cleveland: Arthur C. Clark, 1924.

Rothery, Agnes. *Family Album.* New York: Dodd, 1942.

Rusk, Ralph Leslie. *The Literature of the Middle Western Frontier.* New York: Columbia University Press, 1962.

Salter, Mary Ann. "Quarreling in the English Settlement: The Flowers in Court." *Journal of the Illinois State Historical Society* 75.2 (Summer, 1982).

———. "Morris Birkbeck's Empire on the Prairie Speculation, Philanthropy, or Mania." In *Selected Papers in Illinois History.* Edited by Bruce D. Cady. Springfield: Illinois State Historical Society, 1981.

Stuart, James. *Three Years in North America.* Edinburgh, 1833. Vol. 2 (printed in 2 vol.), printed for Rob't Cadell, Edinburgh and Whittaker & Company, London.

Sutton, Robert P., ed. *The Prairie State.* Grand Rapids, Michigan: William B. Eerdmans, 1976.

Taylor, Anne. *Visions of Harmony.* Oxford: Clarendon Press, 1987.

Tingley, Donald. "Anti-Intellectualism on the Illinois Frontier." *Essays in Illinois History.* Edited by Donald Tingley. Carbondale: Southern Illinois University Press, 1968.

Trollope, Frances. *Domestic Manners of the Americans.* Barre, Massachusetts: The Imprint Society, 1969.

Tyler, Alice Felt. *Freedom's Ferment.* Minneapolis: University of Minnesota Press, 1944, reprinted New York: Harper and Row, 1962.

Walton, Clyde C. *An Illinois Reader.* DeKalb: Northern Illinois University Press, 1970.

Warder, Jeremiah. Letter to Edward Flower, 19 November 1827. Chicago Historical Society, Manuscripts, Flower Family Papers.

Welby, Adlard. *A Visit to North America and the English Settlements in Illinois.* Stamford and Lincoln, Adlard Welby, Esq. Printed for J. K. Drury, 36 Lombard Street. Reprinted in *Early Western Travels,* Vol. 12. Edited by Reuben Gold Thwaites. Cleveland, Ohio, 1905.

Wheeler, Adade Mitchell, and Marlene Stein Wortman. *The Roads They Made, Women in Illinois History.* Chicago: Charles H. Kerr, 1977.

Woods, John. *Two Years Residence in the Settlement on the English Prairie.* London, 1822. Printed for Longman, Hurst, Rees, Orme & Brown, Paternoster Row. Also Thwaite, Vol. 10. New York: AMS Press, 1966.